INTERMEDIATE TO LATE INTERMEDIATE

Great American Songbook

DAN COATES POPULAR PIANO LIBRARY

Produced by
Alfred Music
P.O. Box 10003
Van Nuys, CA 91410-0003
alfred.com

Printed in USA.

ISBN-10: 1-4706-2341-2
ISBN-13: 978-1-4706-2341-8

FOREWORD

The phrase "Great American Songbook" is used to describe the most influential and enduring songs from the early 20th century. Originating largely from Broadway musicals and Hollywood films, these compositions are regarded as some of the most important popular music ever written. This edition revisits many of those songs, casting them in the rich voice of the piano. Standards by legendary songwriters are included: "Someone to Watch Over Me" and "They Can't Take That Away from Me" by George and Ira Gershwin; "My Funny Valentine" and "The Lady Is a Tramp" by Richard Rodgers and Lorenz Hart; "Skylark" by Hoagy Carmichael; and "I Get a Kick Out of You" and "I've got You Under My Skin" by Cole Porter. The bluesy chords of "Cry Me a River," the evocative melody of "The Days of Wine and Roses," and all of the other wonderful musical moments are an essential addition to the Popular Piano Library.

Since 1976, Dan Coates has arranged thousands of popular music titles. Composers and artists such as John Williams, Burt Bacharach, and Elton John have expressed total confidence in Dan's ability to create outstanding piano arrangements that retain the essence of the original music. He has arranged everything from movie, television, and Broadway themes to chart-topping pop and rock titles. In addition to creating piano arrangements for players of all levels, Dan also composes original music for student pianists.

CONTENTS

Anything Goes 10

Cry Me a River 4

The Days of Wine and Roses 8

Dream a Little Dream of Me 13

Embraceable You 16

Falling In Love with Love 19

Fools Rush In 24

I Get a Kick Out of You 27

I Got Rhythm 32

I Only Have Eyes for You 38

I'm in the Mood for Love 35

In the Still of the Night 42

It Had to Be You 47

I've Got You Under My Skin 50

The Lady Is a Tramp 55

Long Ago (And Far Away) 60

Love Is Here to Stay 63

Make Someone Happy 66

My Funny Valentine 69

On the Street Where You Live 72

The Shadow of Your Smile 75

Singin' in the Rain 78

Skylark 81

So In Love 84

Someone to Watch Over Me 89

Stardust 92

Summertime 96

They Can't Take That Away from Me 100

When I Fall In Love 103

Where or When 106

With a Song in My Heart 110

You'll Never Know 113

Cry Me a River

Words and Music by Arthur Hamilton
Arr. Dan Coates

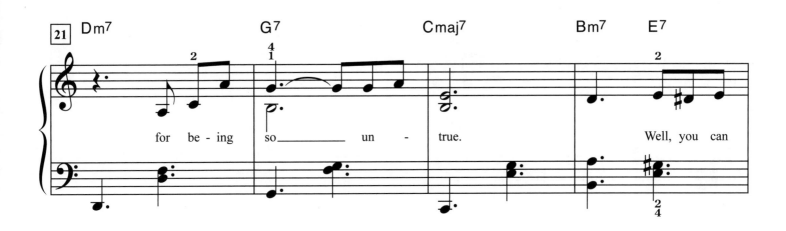

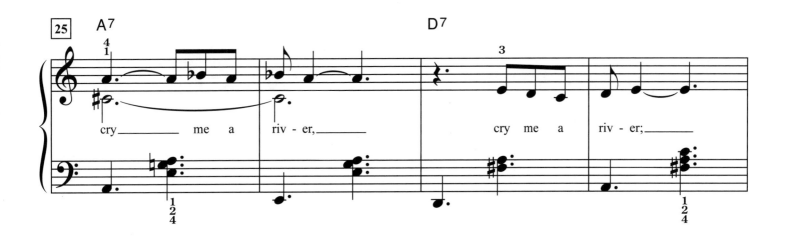

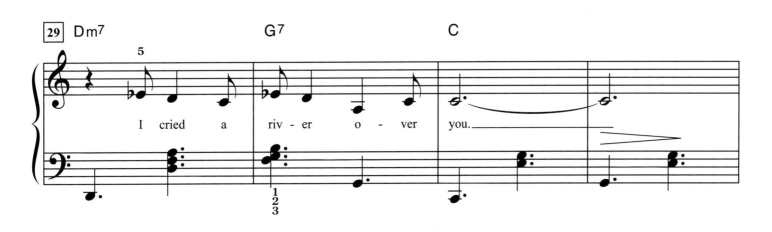

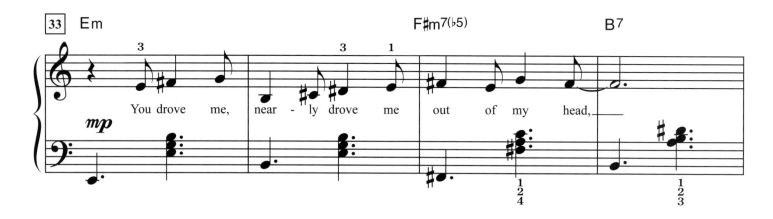

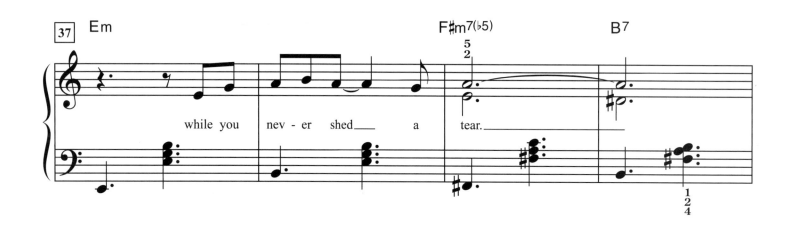

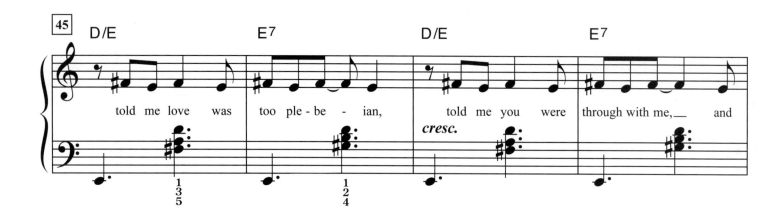

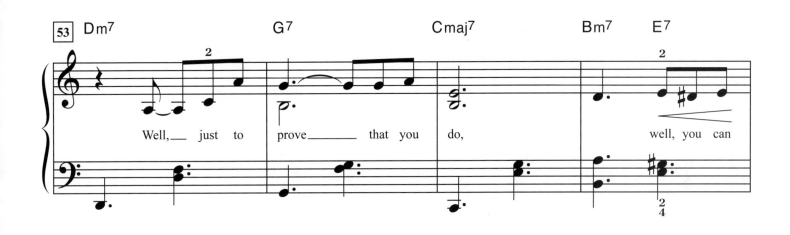

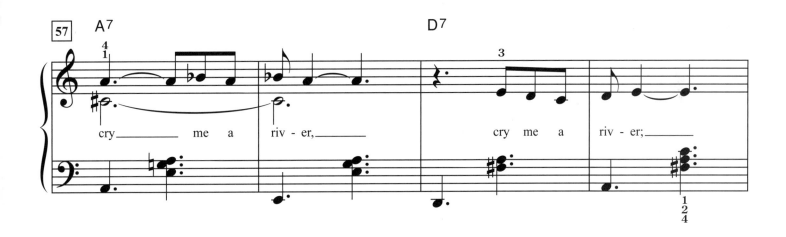

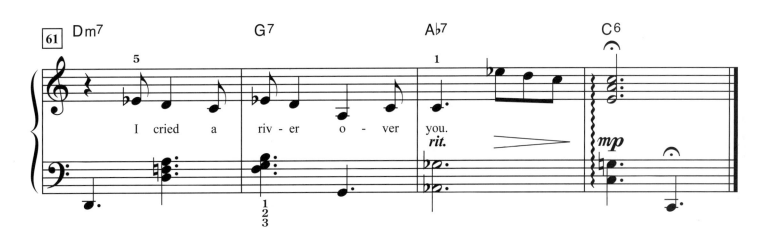

The Days of Wine and Roses

Lyrics by Johnny Mercer
Music by Henry Mancini
Arr. Dan Coates

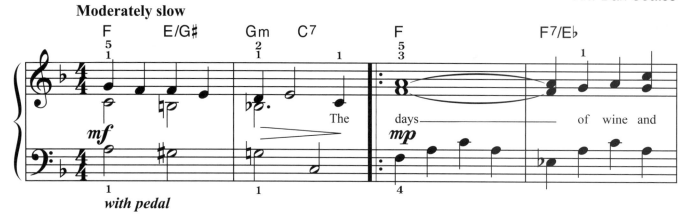

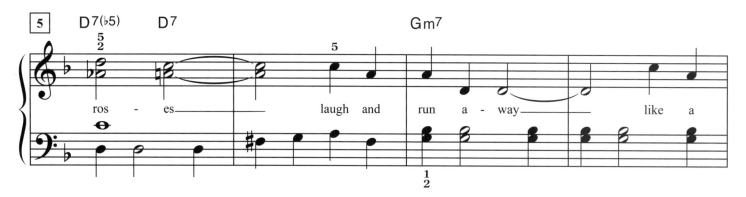

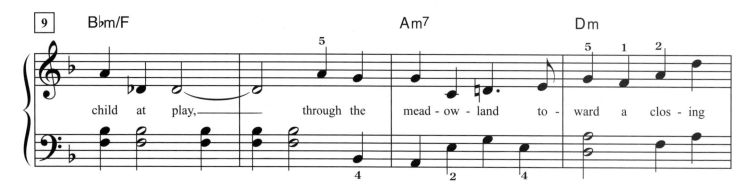

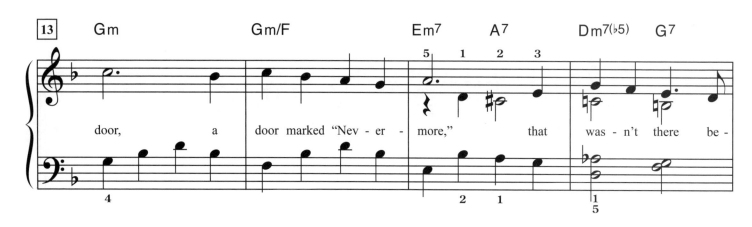

Anything Goes

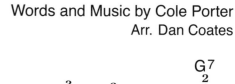

Words and Music by Cole Porter
Arr. Dan Coates

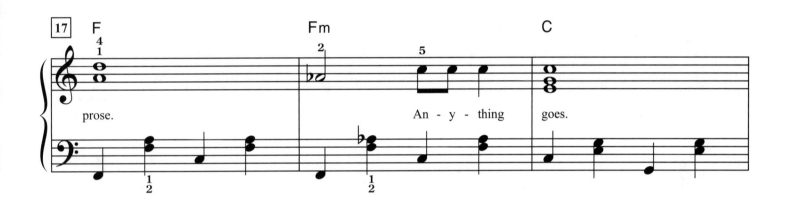

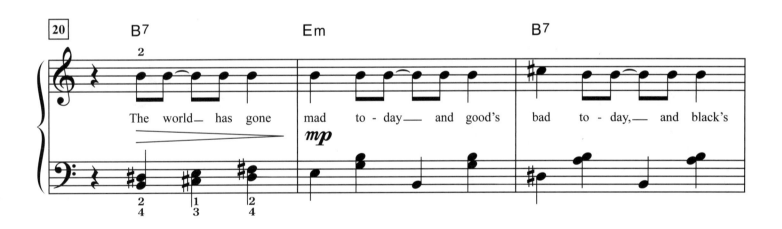

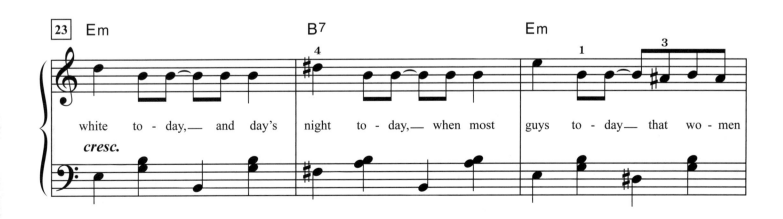

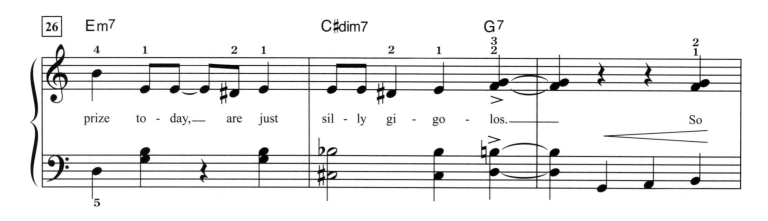

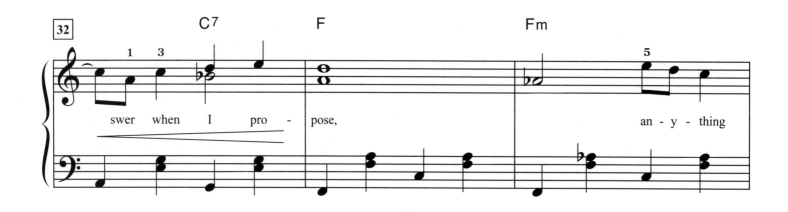

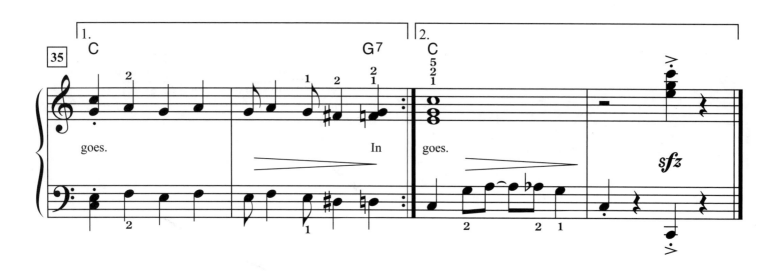

Dream a Little Dream of Me

Lyrics by Gus Kahn
Music by Fabian Andre and Wilbur Schwandt
Arr. Dan Coates

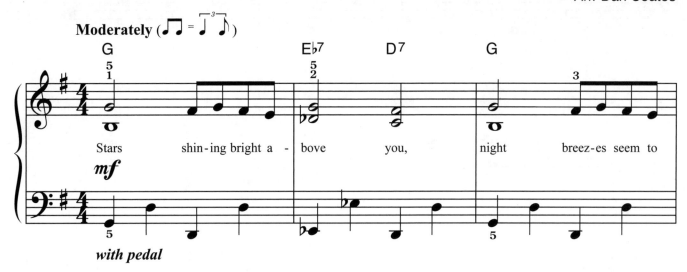

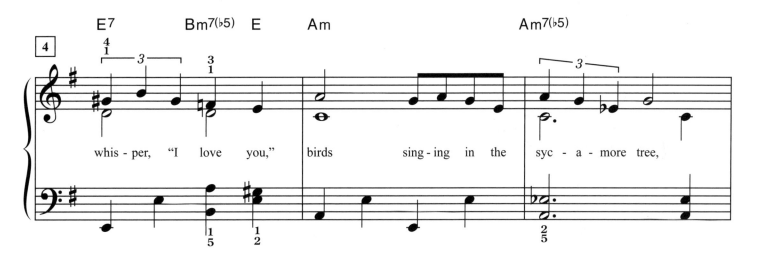

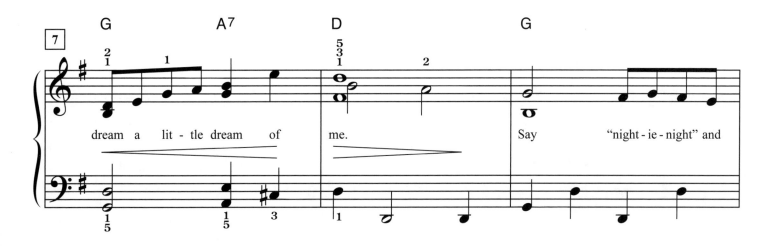

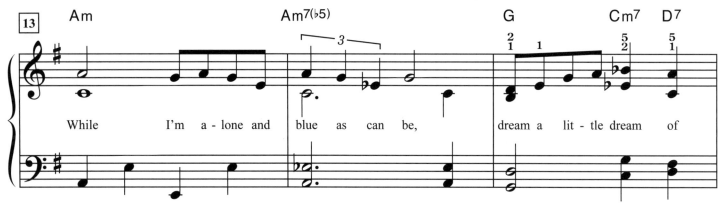

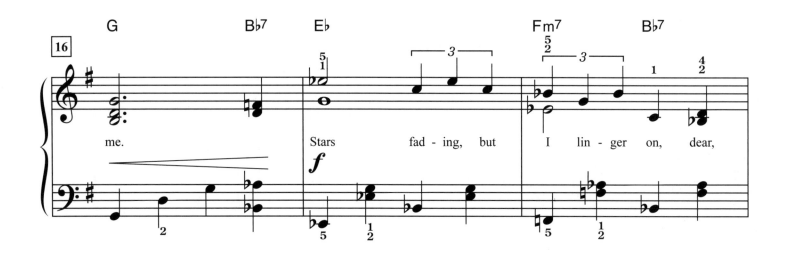

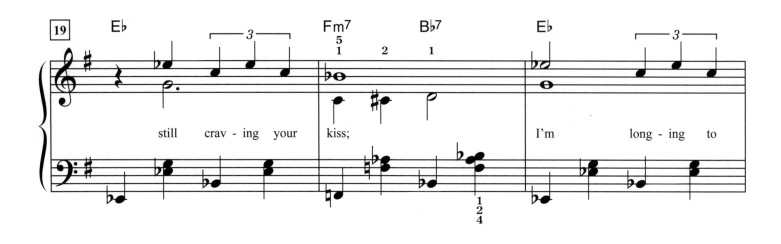

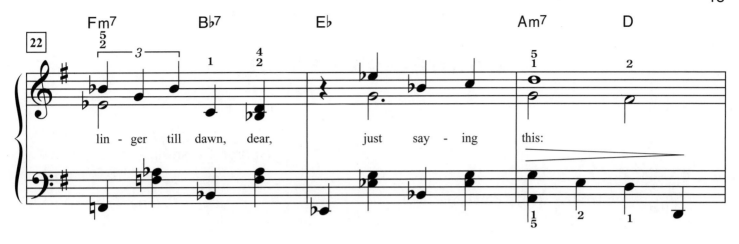

Lyrics: lin - ger till dawn, dear, just say - ing this:

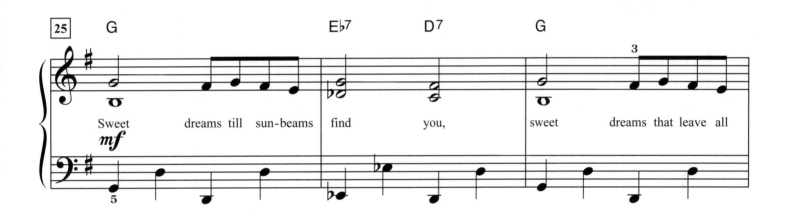

Lyrics: Sweet dreams till sun-beams find you, sweet dreams that leave all

Lyrics: wor - ries be - hind you, but in your dreams, what - ev - er they be,

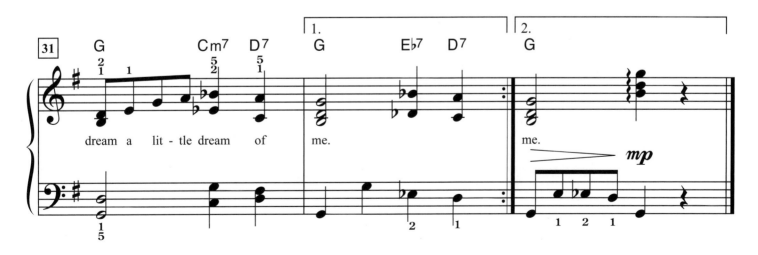

Lyrics: dream a lit - tle dream of me. me.

Embraceable You

Music and Lyrics by
George Gershwin and Ira Gershwin
Arr. Dan Coates

Moderately slow, with expression

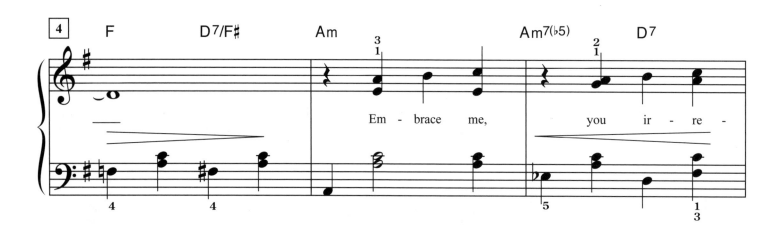

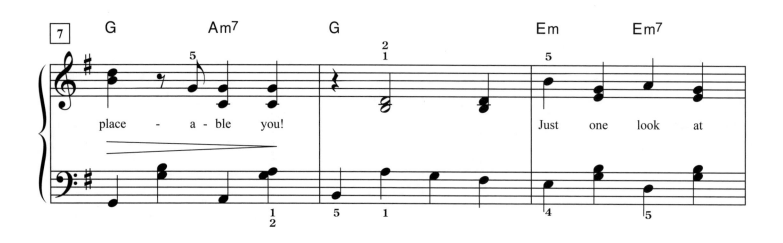

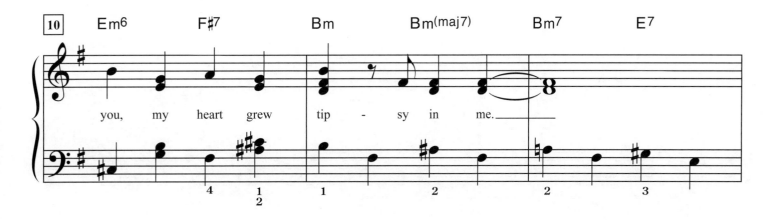

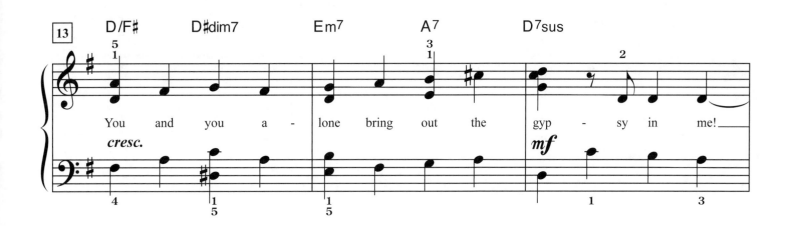

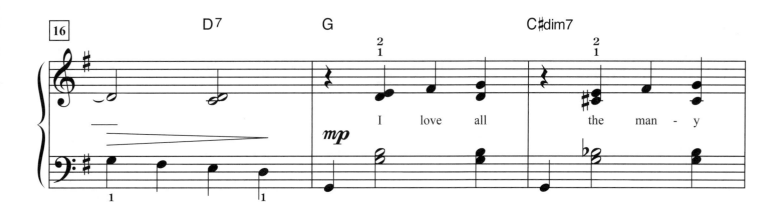

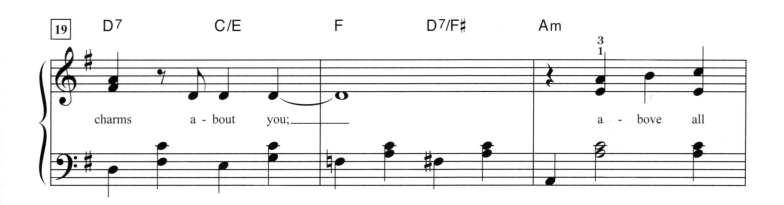

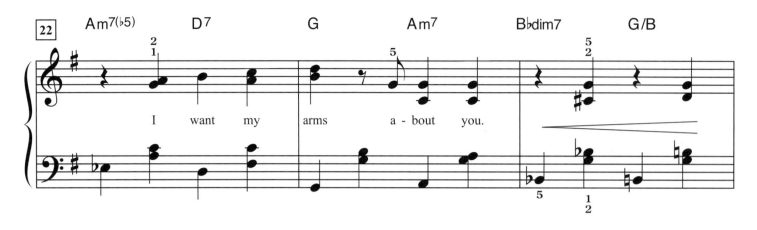

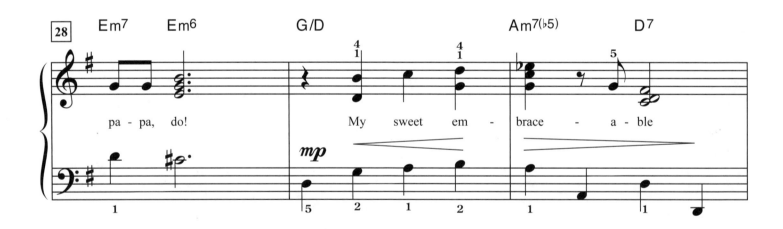

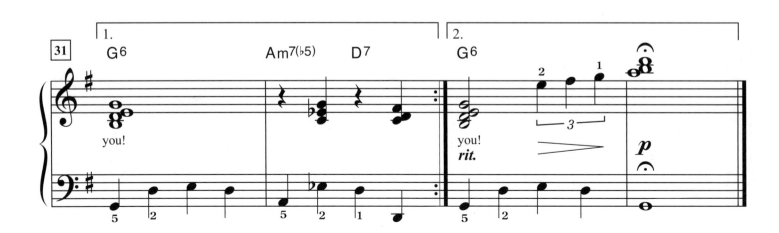

Falling In Love with Love

Words by Lorenz Hart
Music by Richard Rodgers
Arr. Dan Coates

Moderate waltz

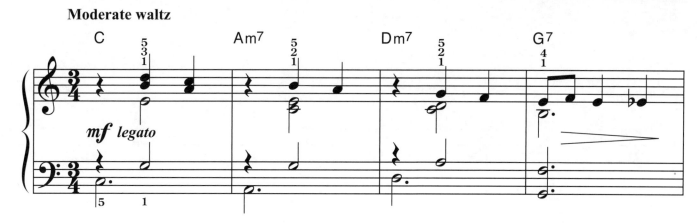

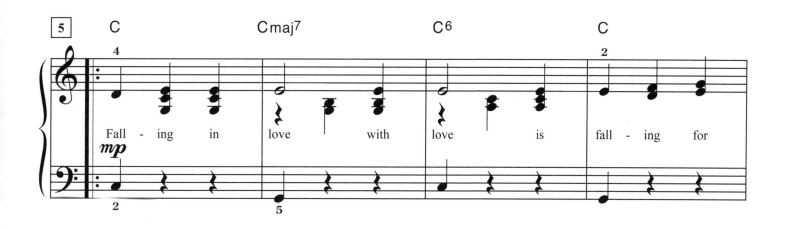

Fall - ing in love with love is fall - ing for

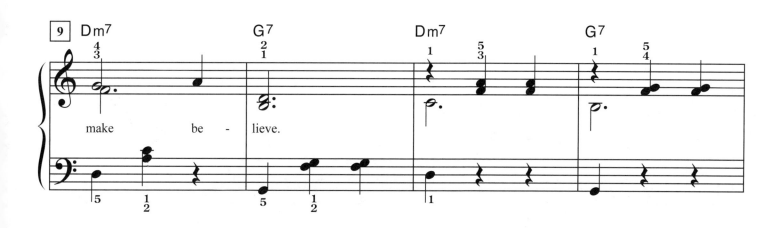

make be - lieve.

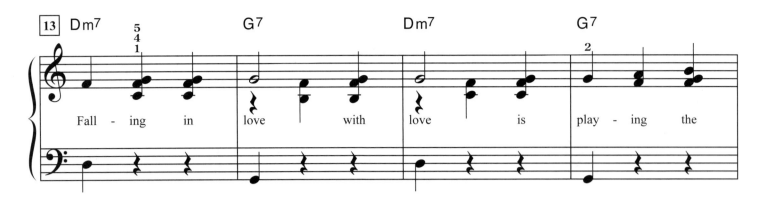

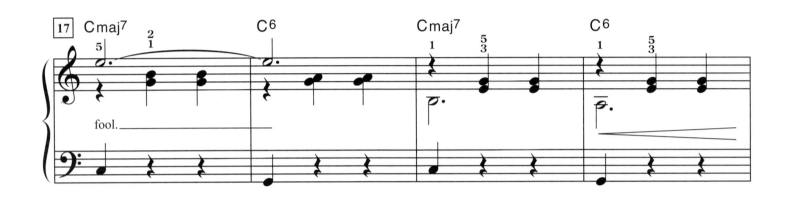

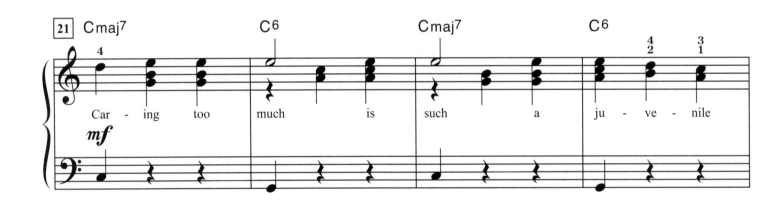

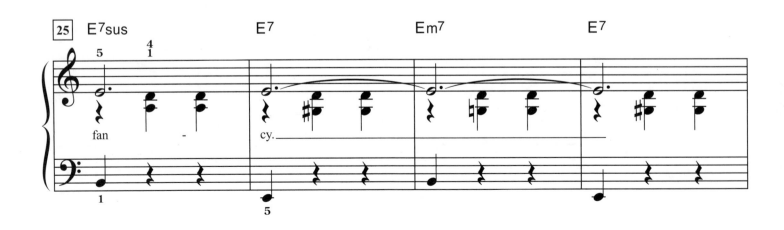

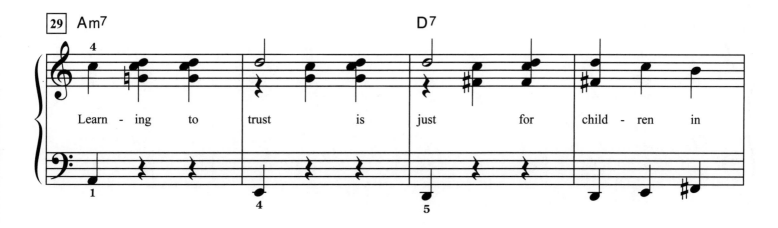

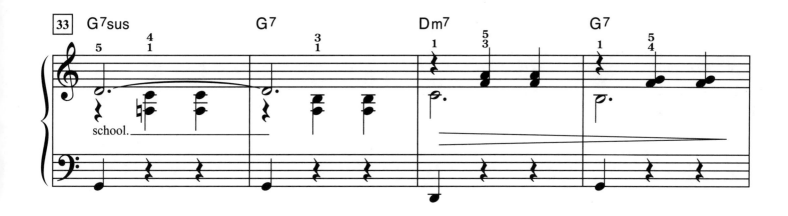

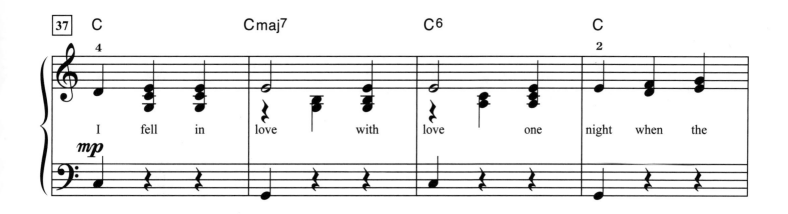

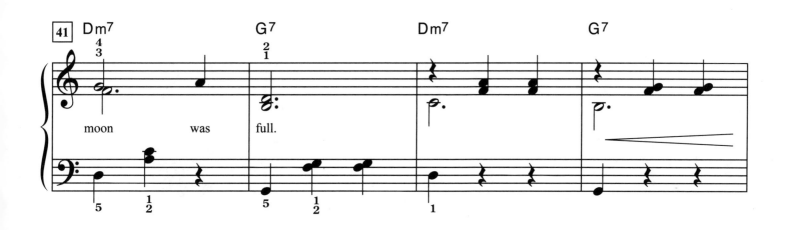

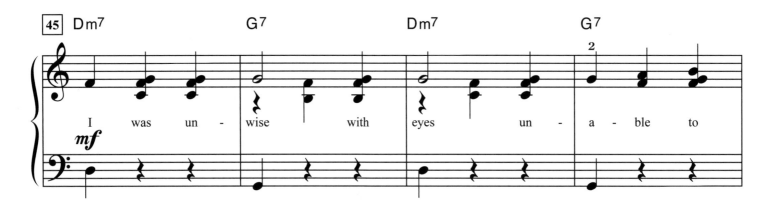

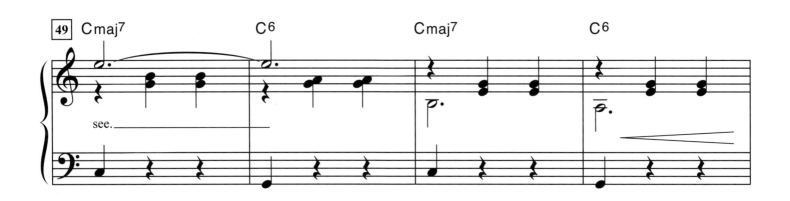

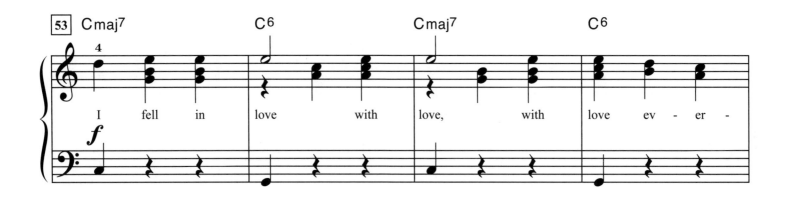

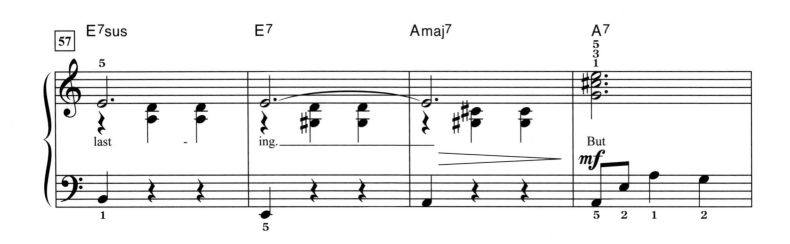

23

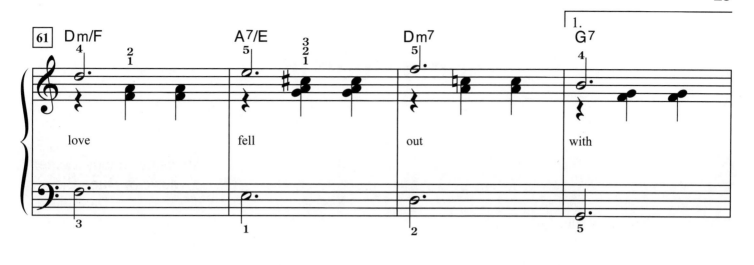

love fell out with

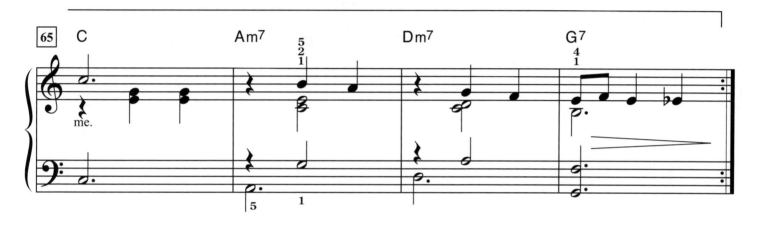

me.

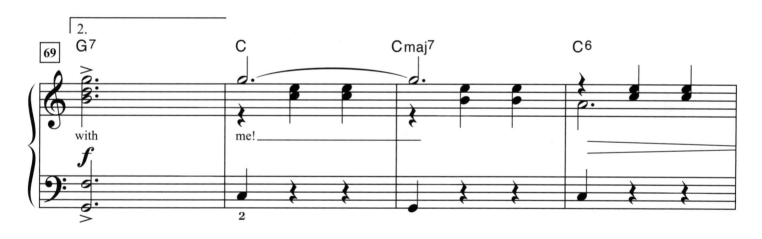

with me!

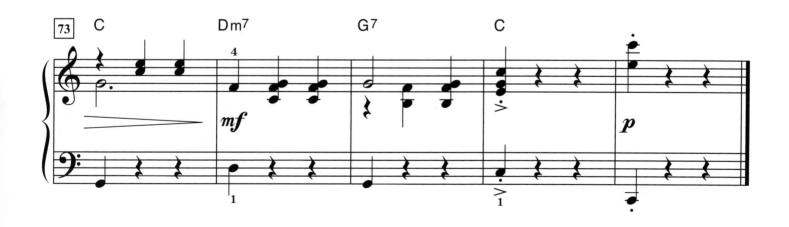

Fools Rush In

Lyrics by Johnny Mercer
Music by Rube Bloom
Arr. Dan Coates

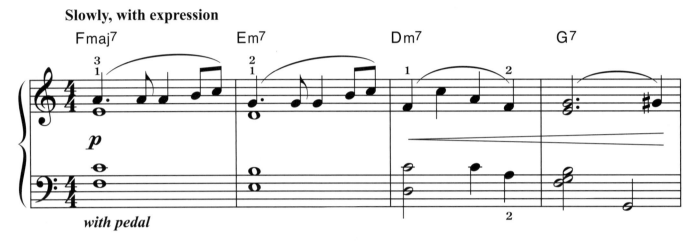

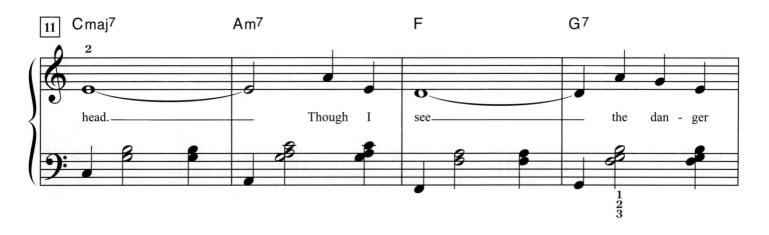

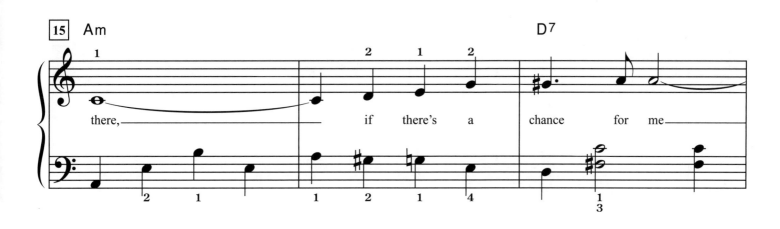

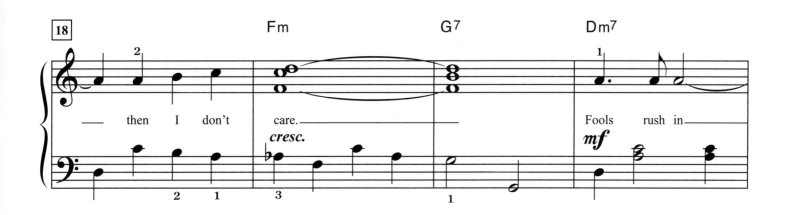

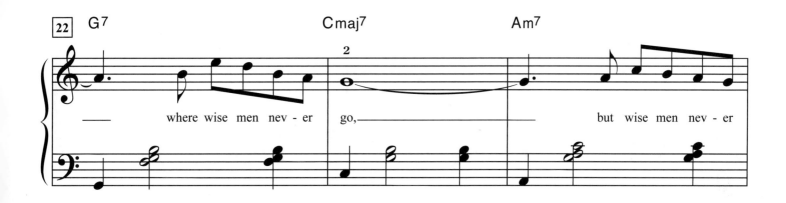

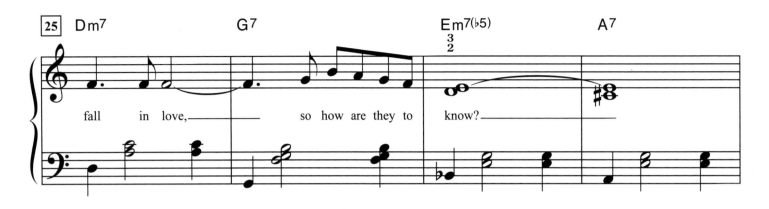

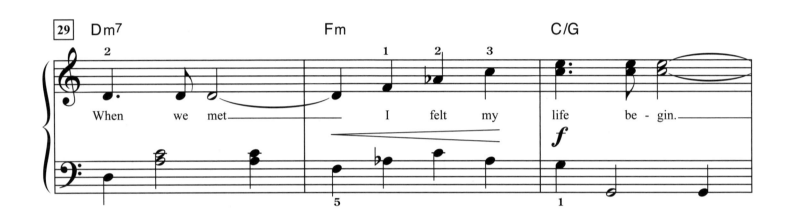

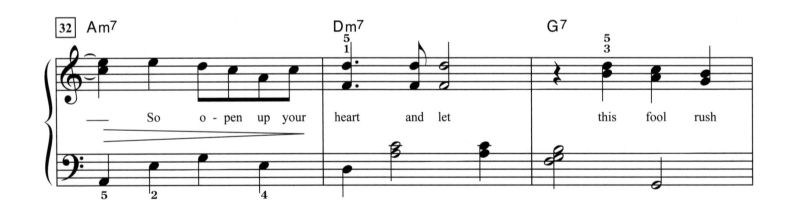

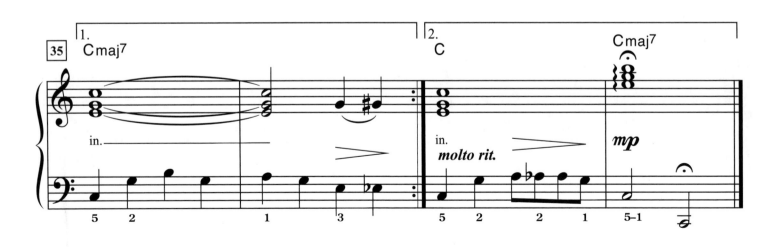

I Get a Kick Out of You

Words and Music by Cole Porter
Arr. Dan Coates

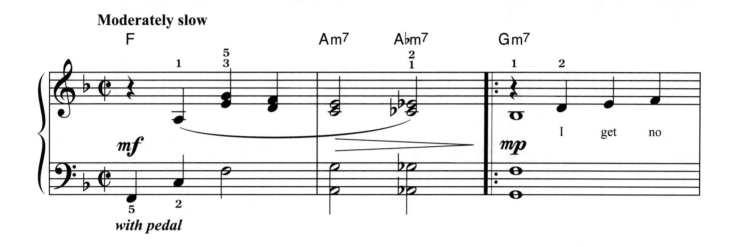

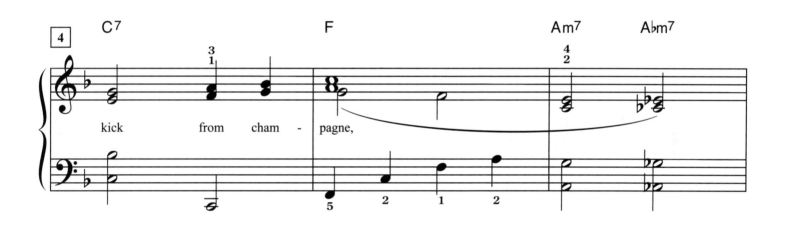

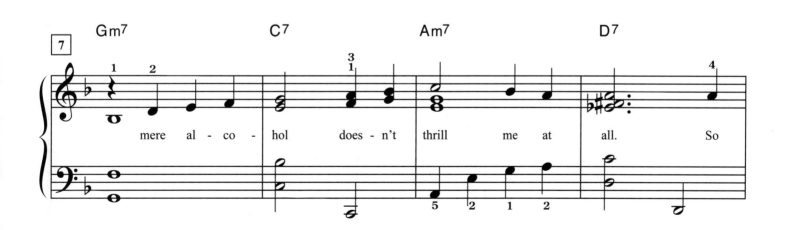

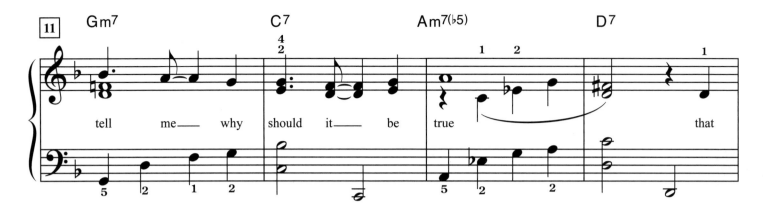

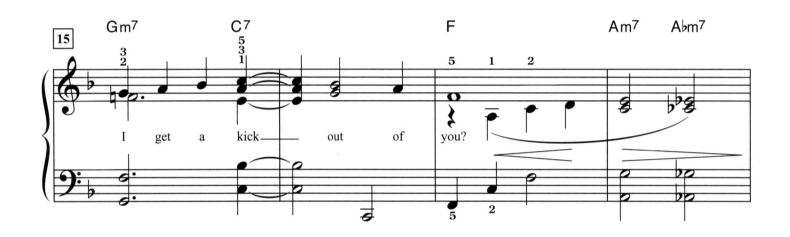

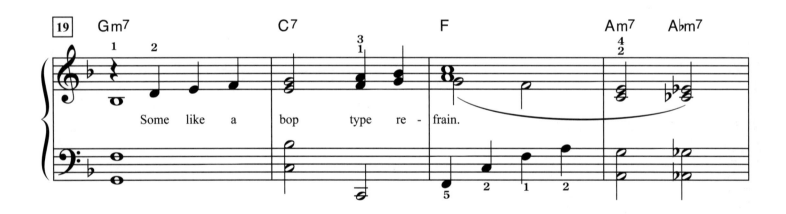

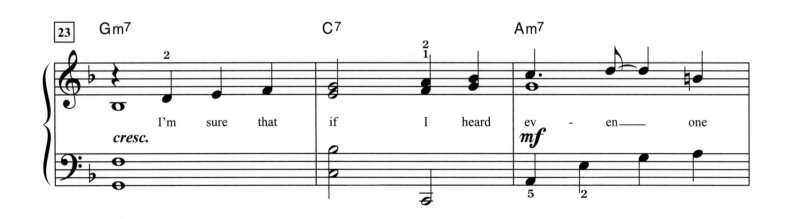

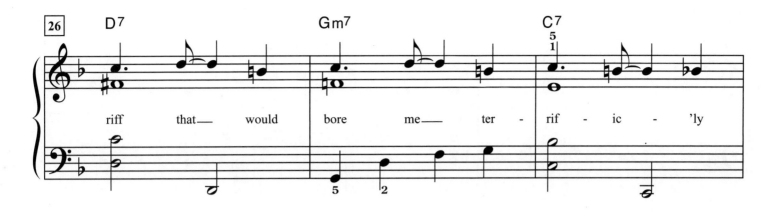

riff that— would bore me— ter - rif - ic - 'ly

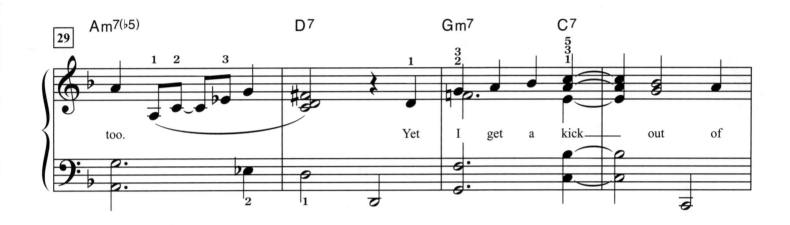

too. Yet I get a kick— out of

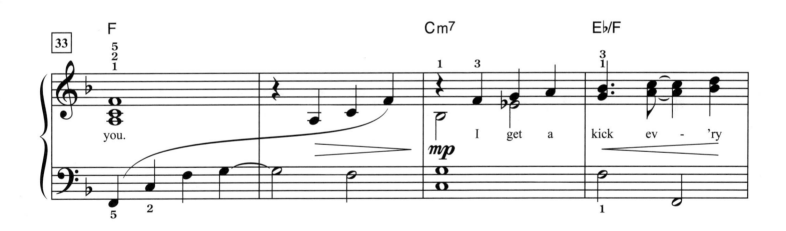

you. I get a kick ev - 'ry

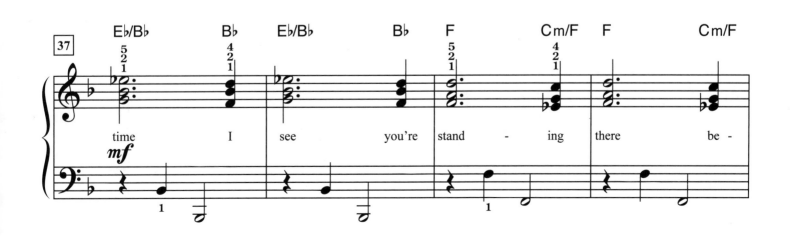

time I see you're stand - ing there be -

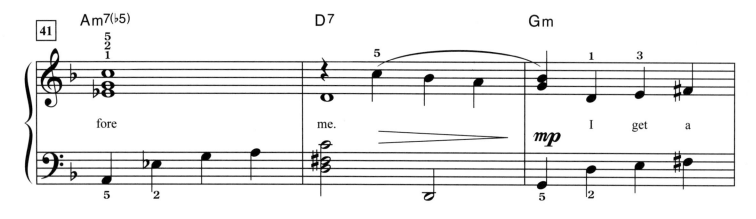

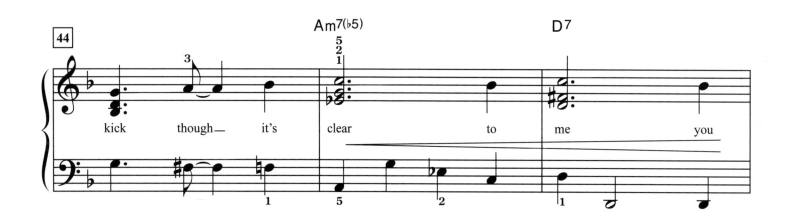

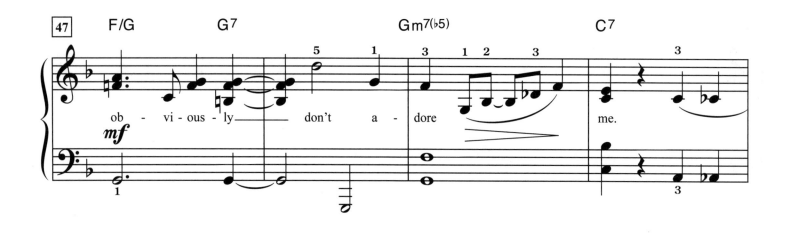

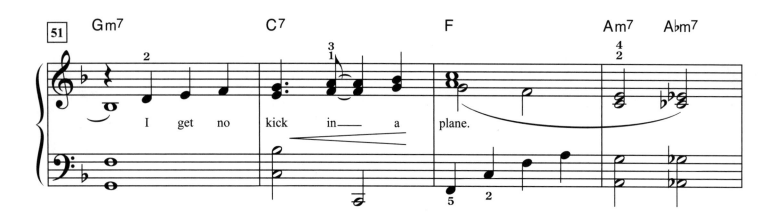

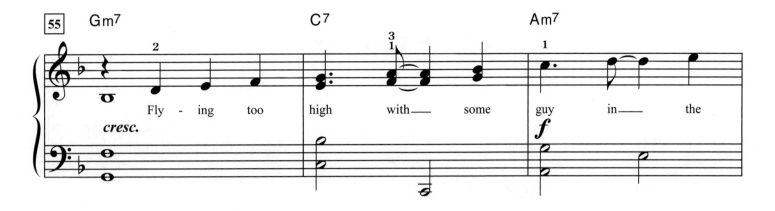

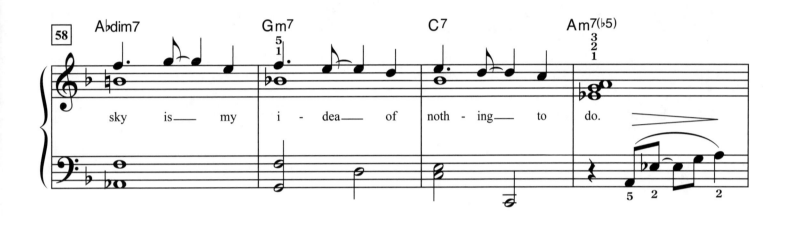

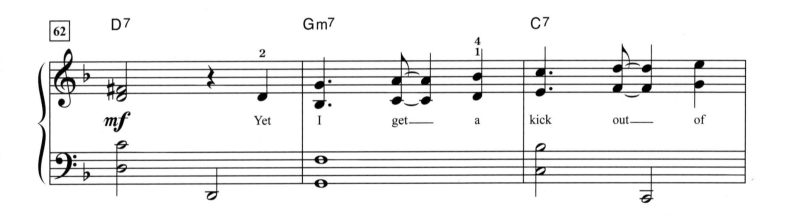

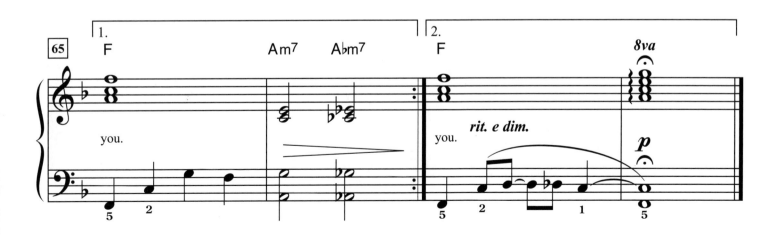

I Got Rhythm

Music and Lyrics by
George Gershwin and Ira Gershwin
Arr. Dan Coates

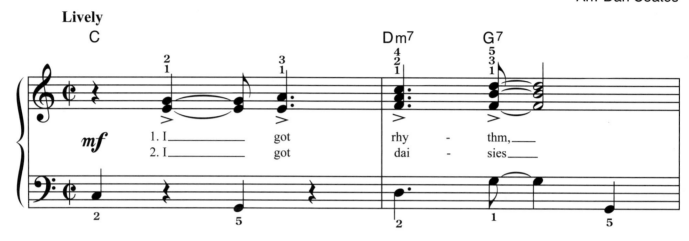

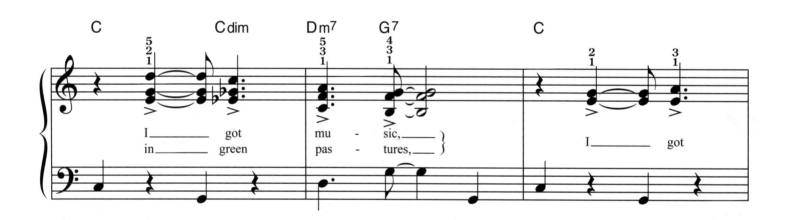

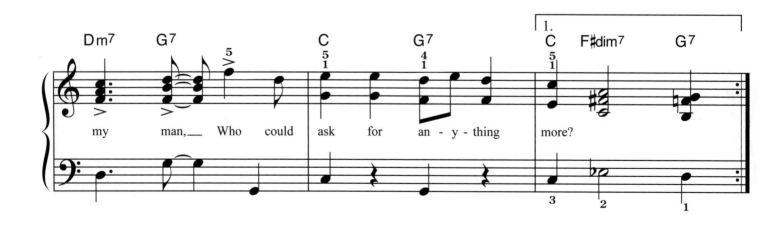

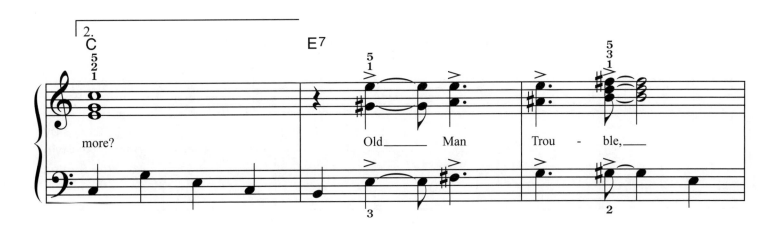

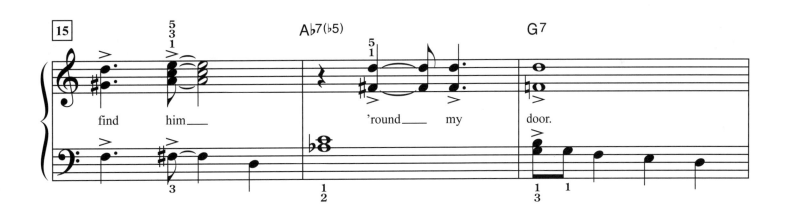

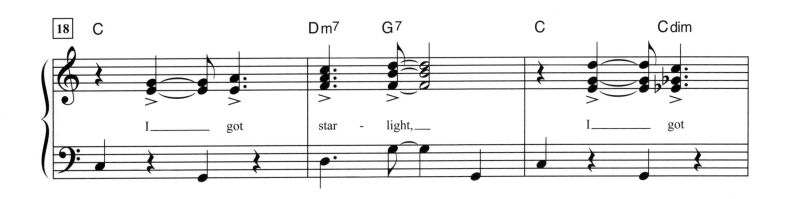

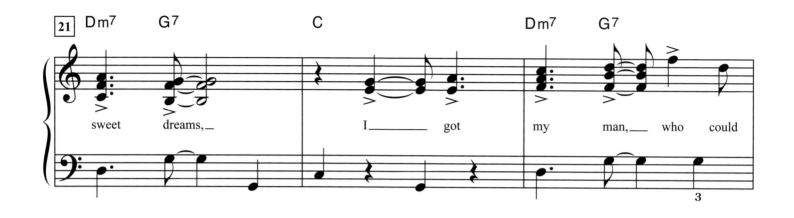

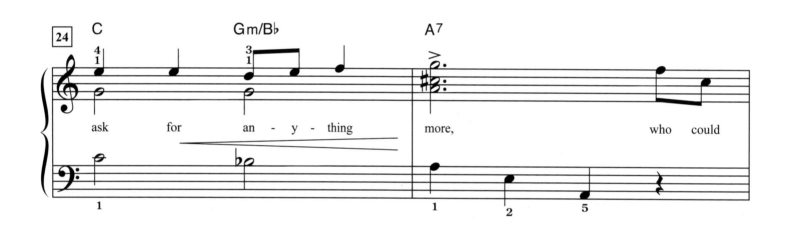

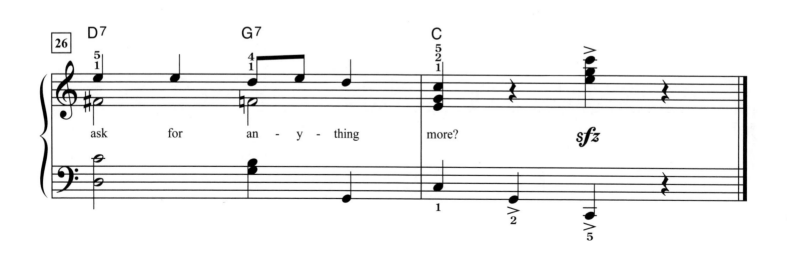

I'm in the Mood for Love

Music by Jimmy McHugh
Lyrics by Dorothy Fields
Arr. Dan Coates

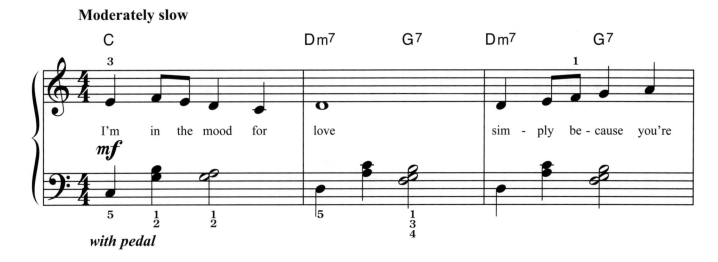

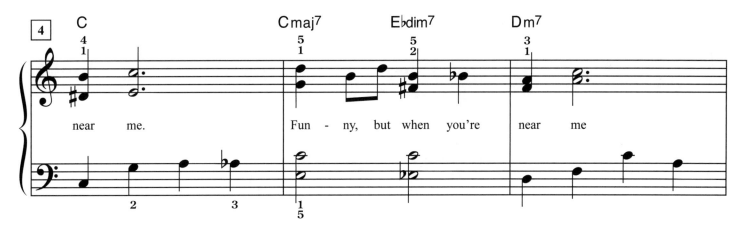

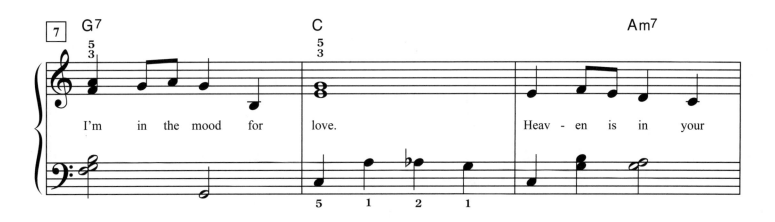

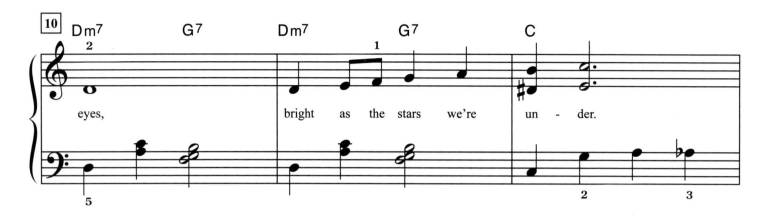

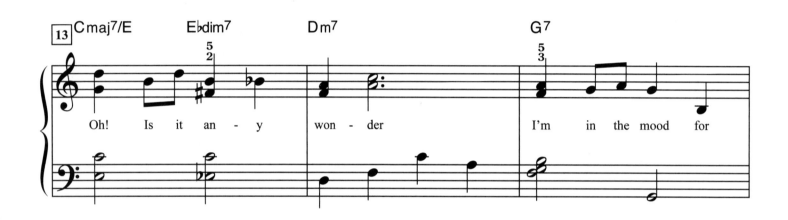

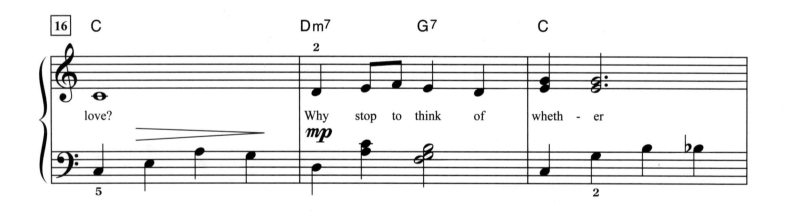

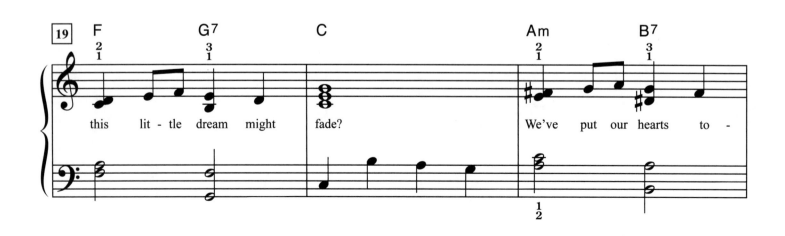

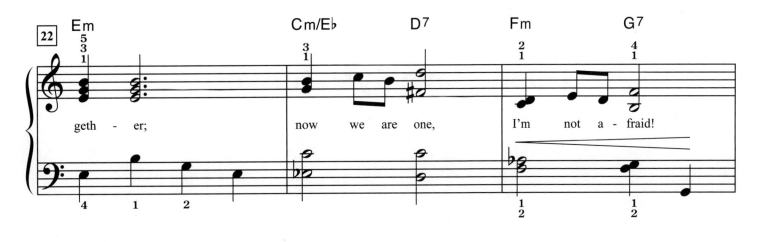

geth - er; now we are one, I'm not a - fraid!

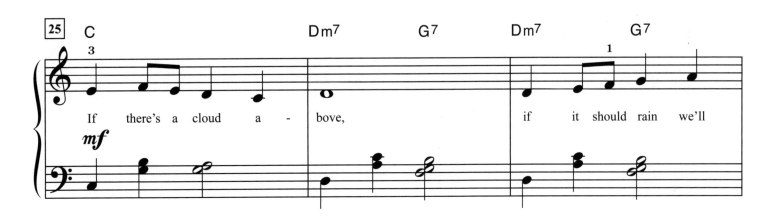

If there's a cloud a - bove, if it should rain we'll

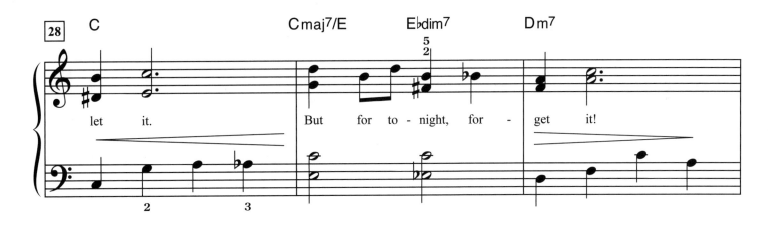

let it. But for to - night, for - get it!

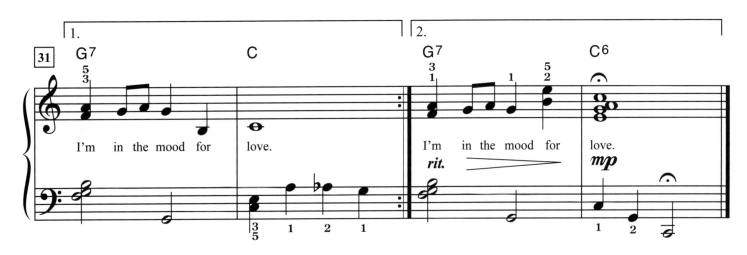

I'm in the mood for love. I'm in the mood for love.

I Only Have Eyes for You

Words by Al Dubin
Music by Harry Warren
Arr. Dan Coates

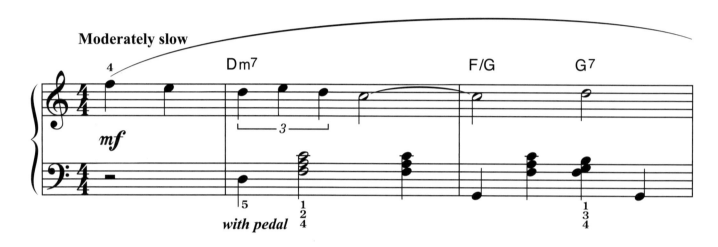

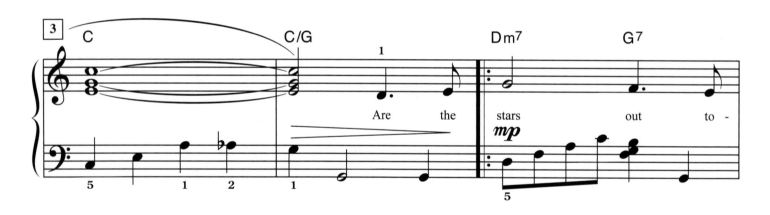

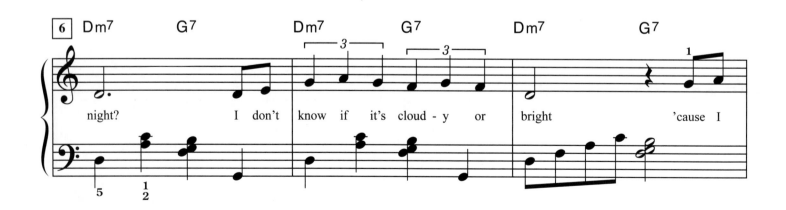

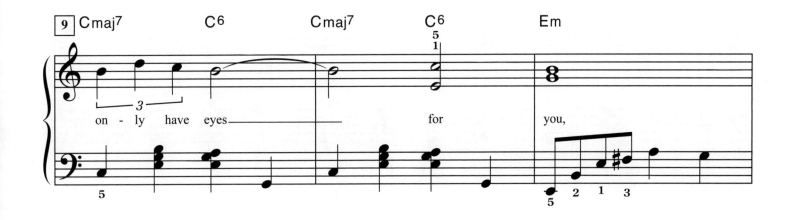

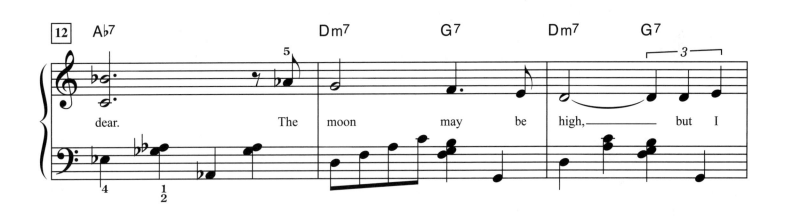

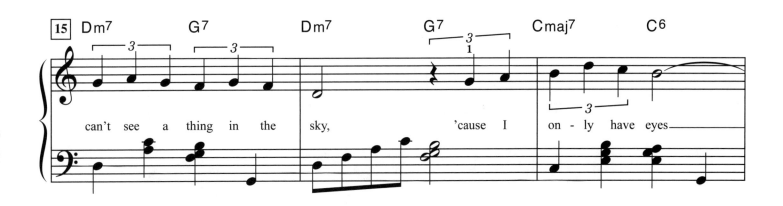

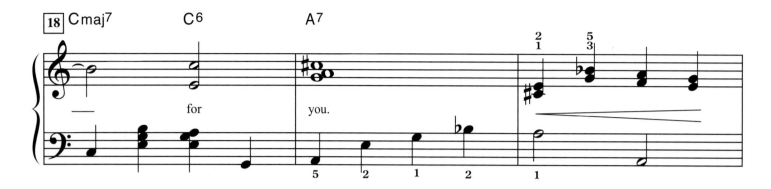

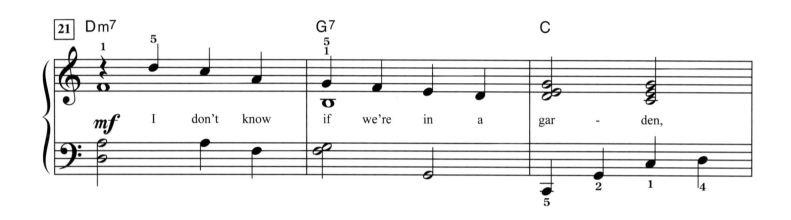

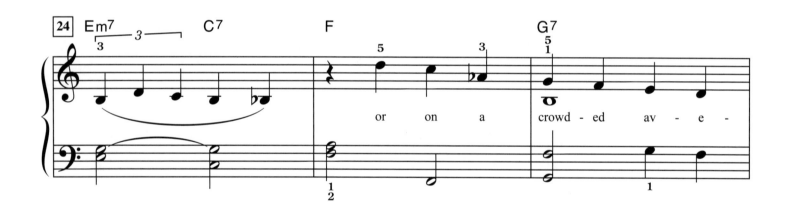

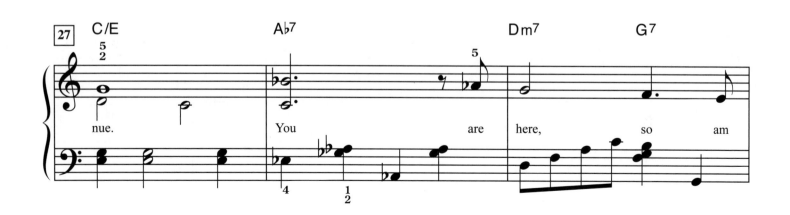

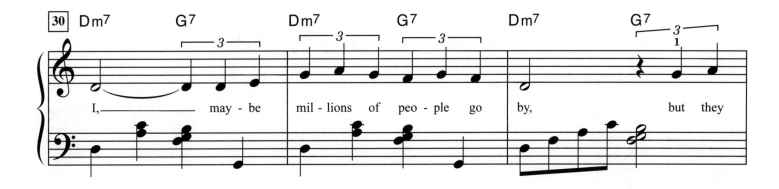

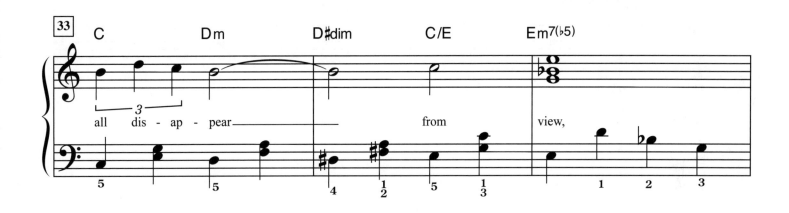

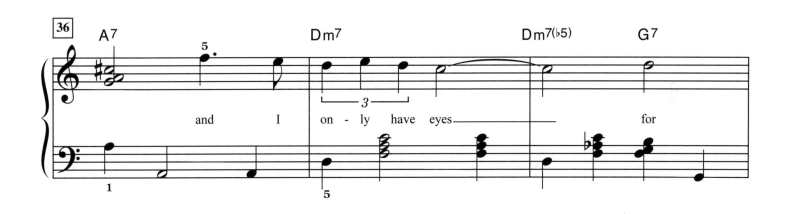

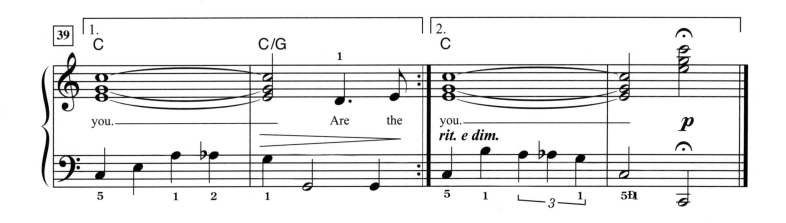

In the Still of the Night

Words and Music by Cole Porter
Arr. Dan Coates

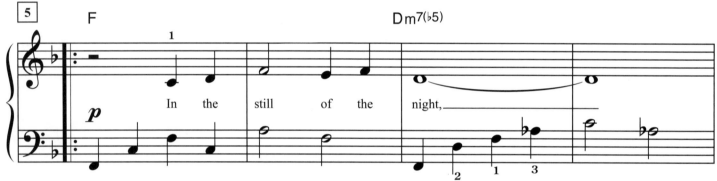

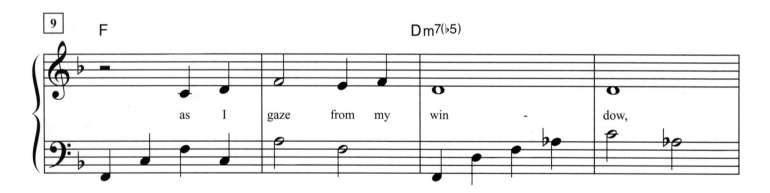

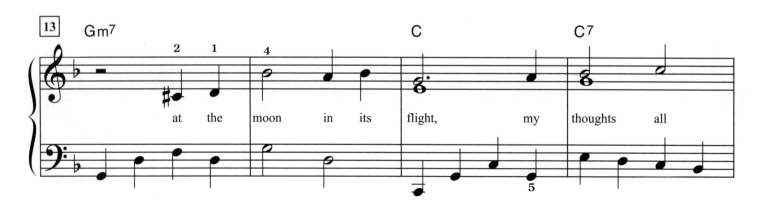

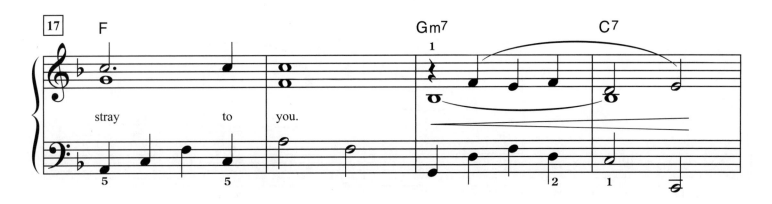

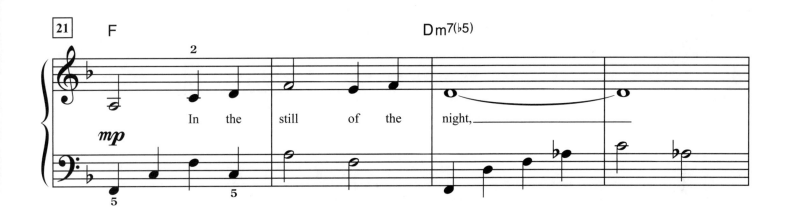

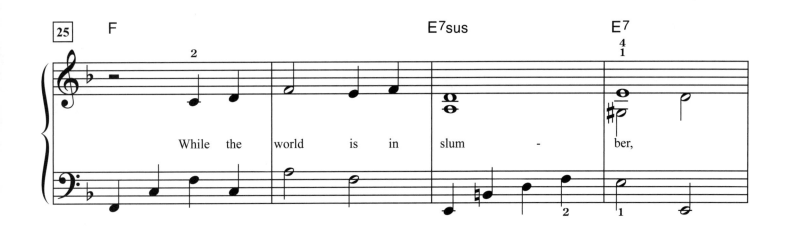

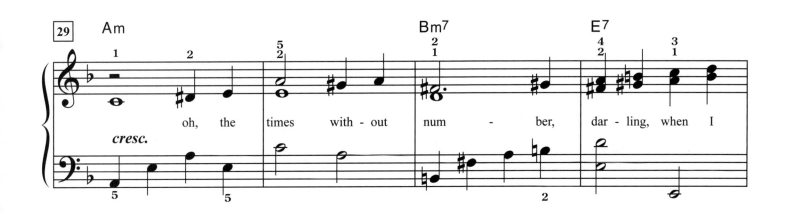

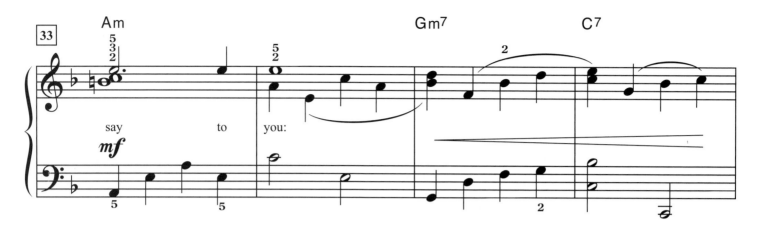

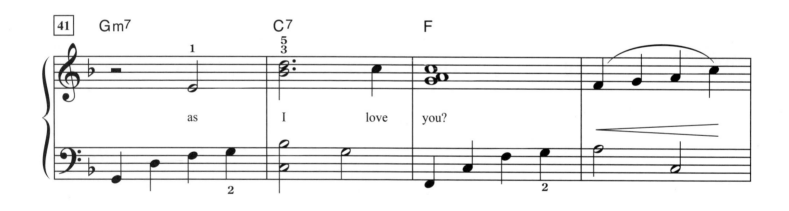

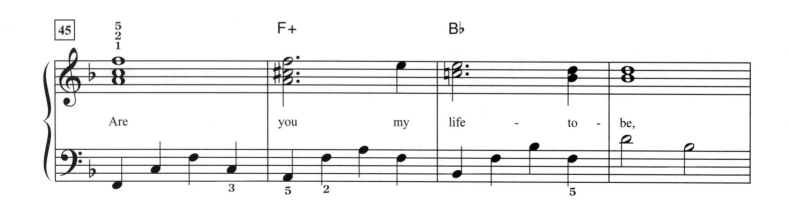

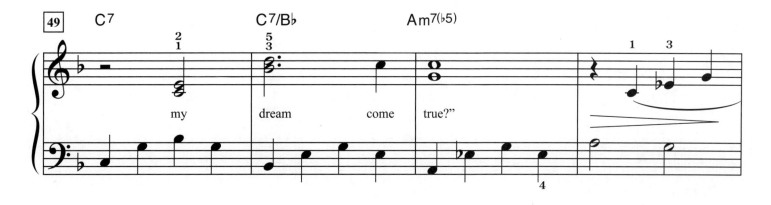

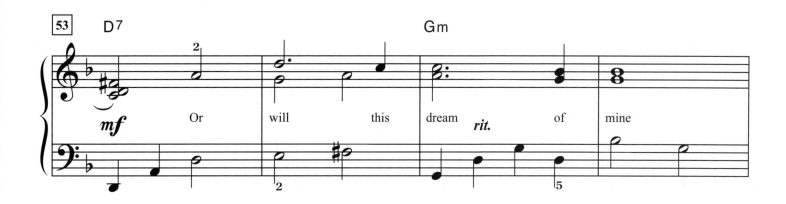

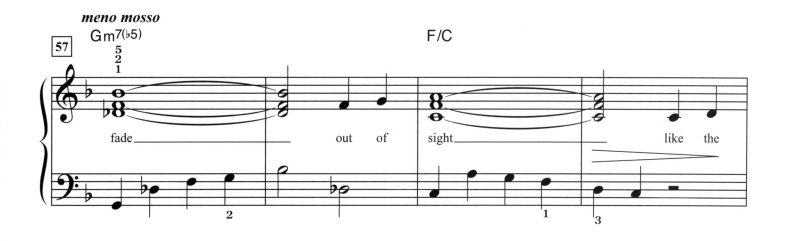

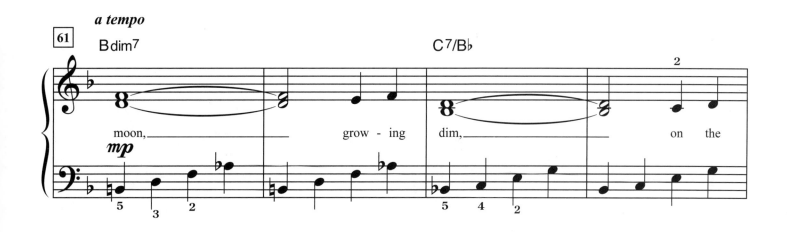

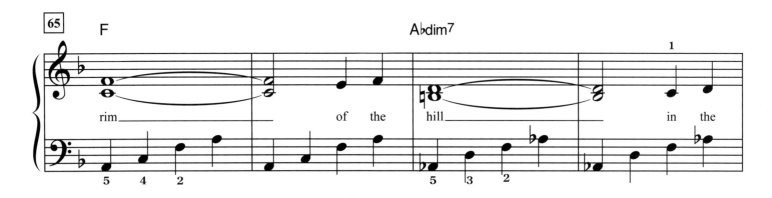

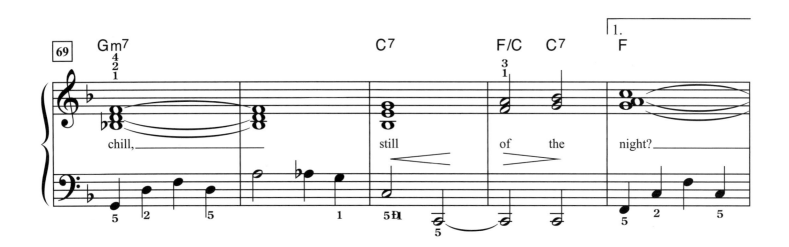

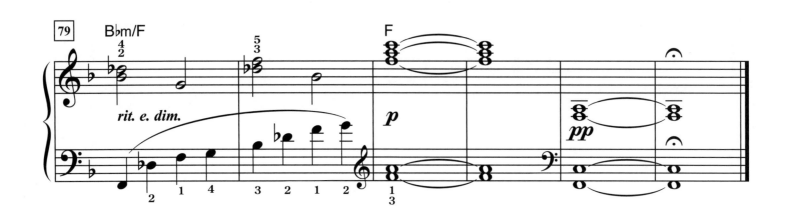

It Had to Be You

Words by Gus Kahn
Music by Isham Jones
Arr. Dan Coates

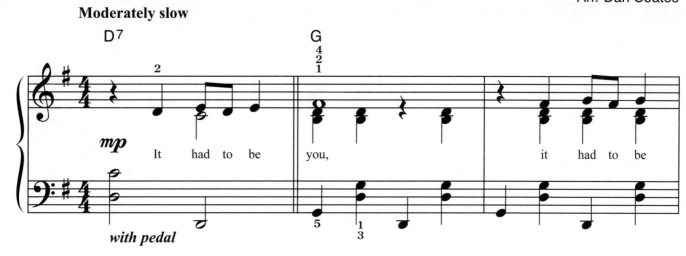

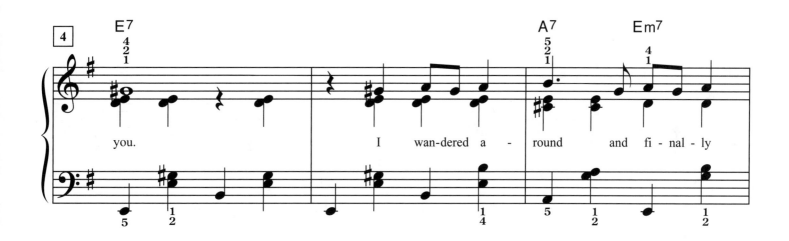

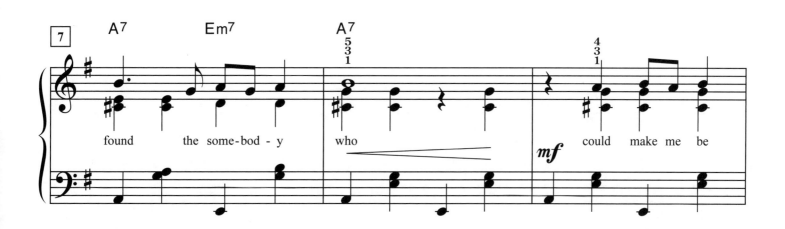

I've Got You Under My Skin

Words and Music by Cole Porter
Arr. Dan Coates

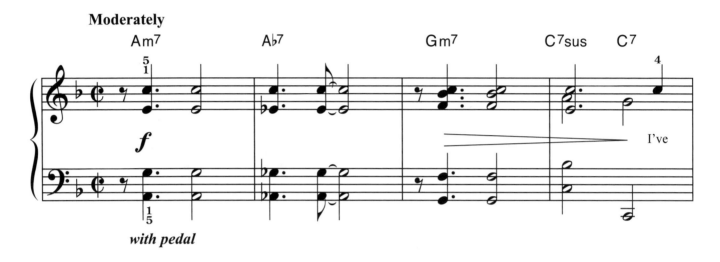

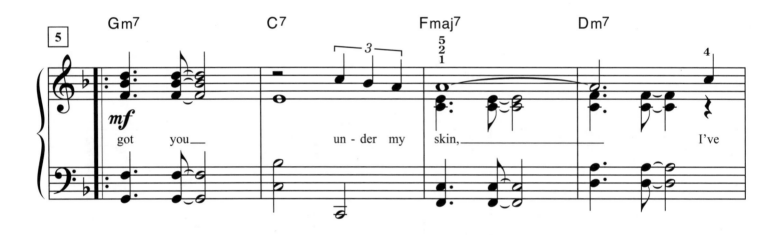

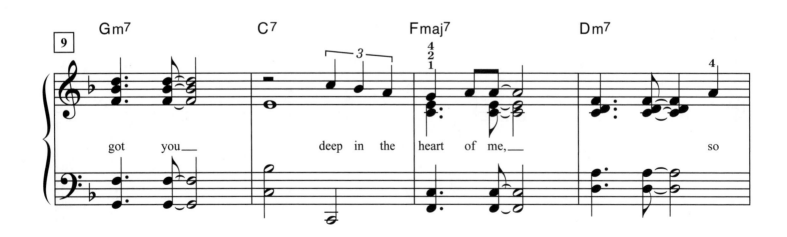

deep in my heart, you're real - ly a part of___ me.___ I've

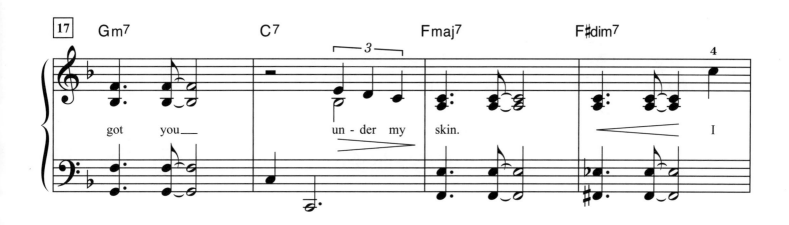

got you___ un - der my skin. I

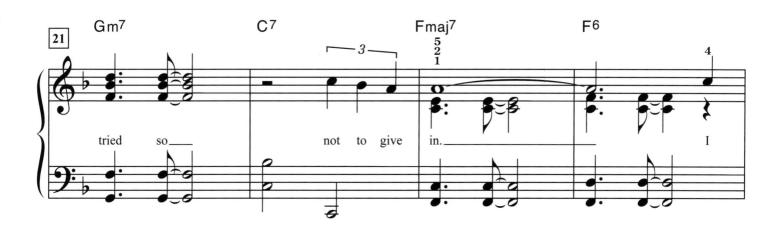

tried so___ not to give in.___ I

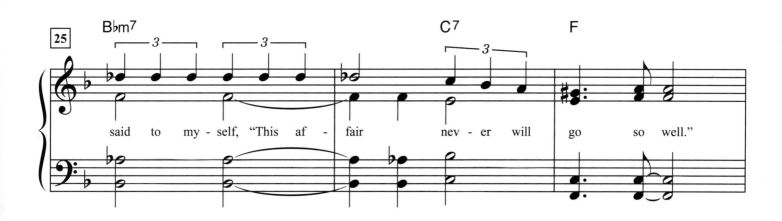

said to my - self, "This af - fair nev - er will go so well."

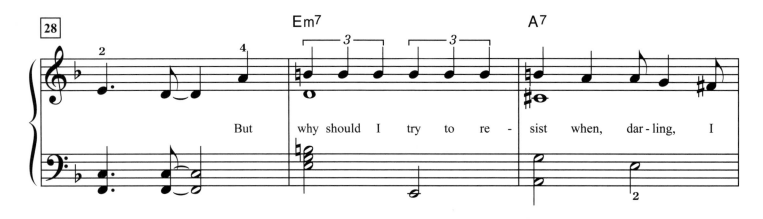

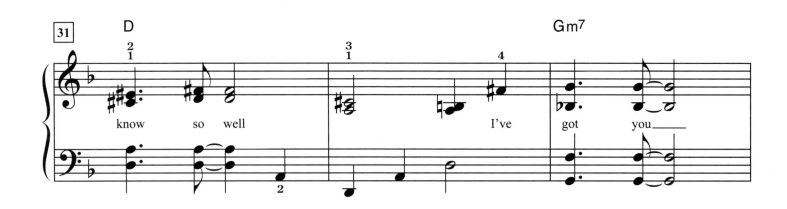

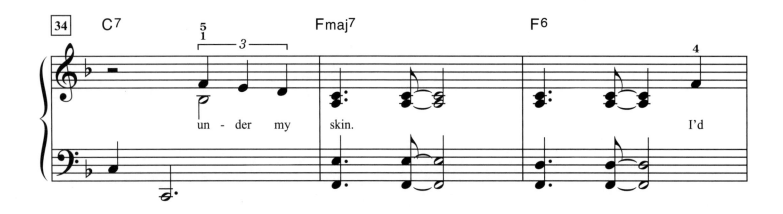

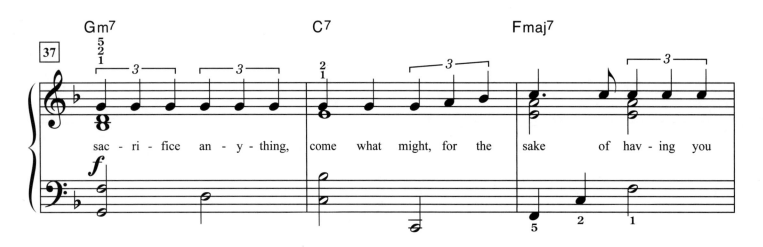

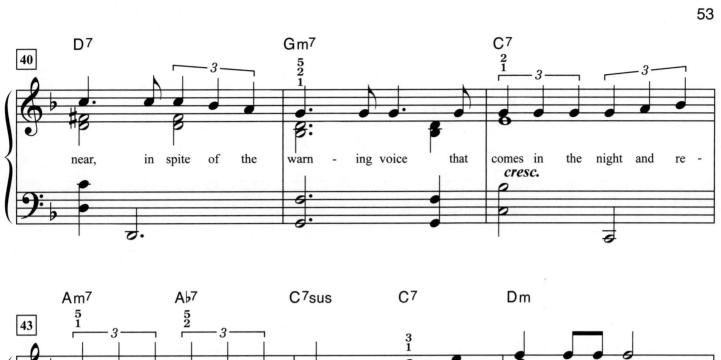

near, in spite of the warn - ing voice that comes in the night and re -

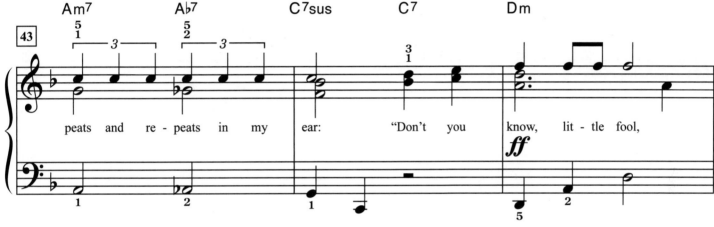

peats and re - peats in my ear: "Don't you know, lit - tle fool,

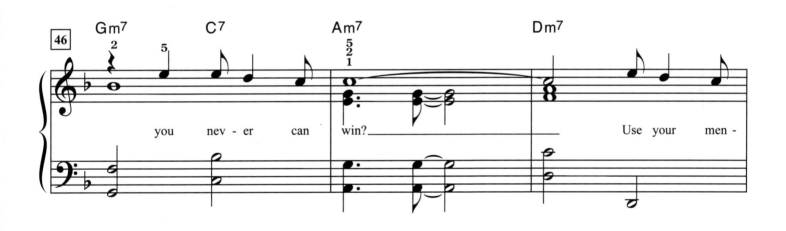

you nev - er can win?_____ Use your men -

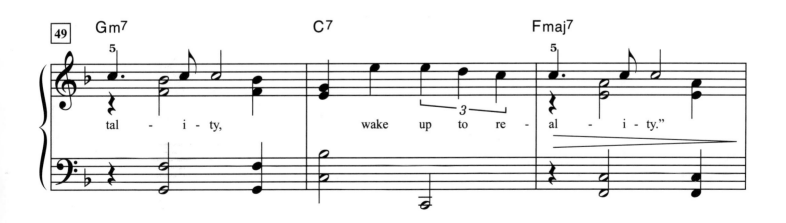

tal - i - ty, wake up to re - al - i - ty."

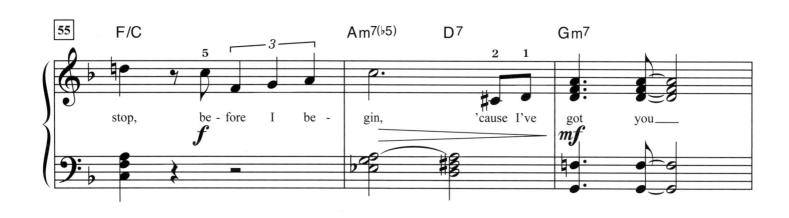

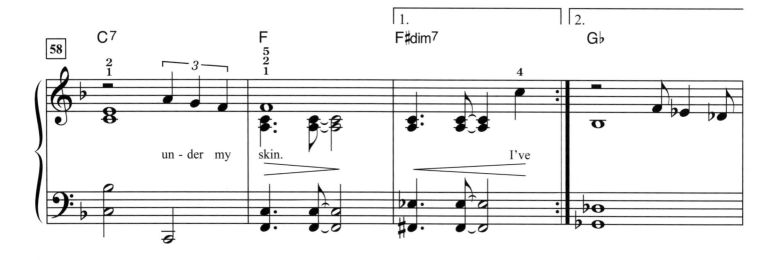

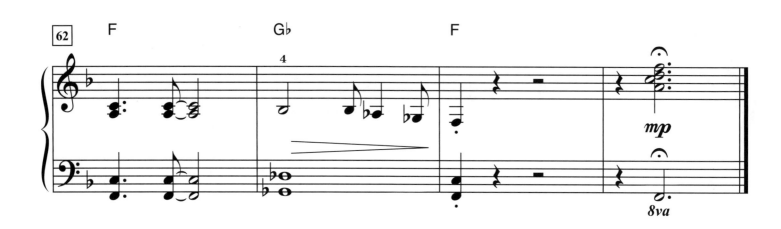

The Lady Is a Tramp

Words by Lorenz Hart
Music by Richard Rodgers
Arr. Dan Coates

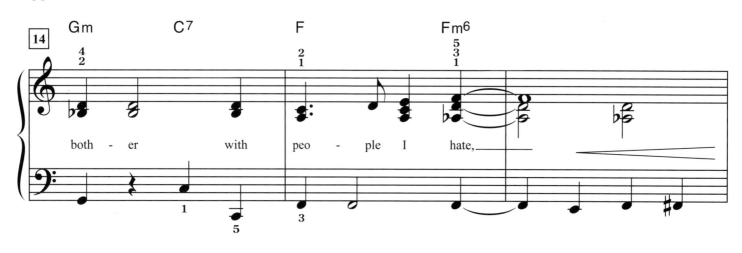

both - er   with   peo - ple   I   hate,____

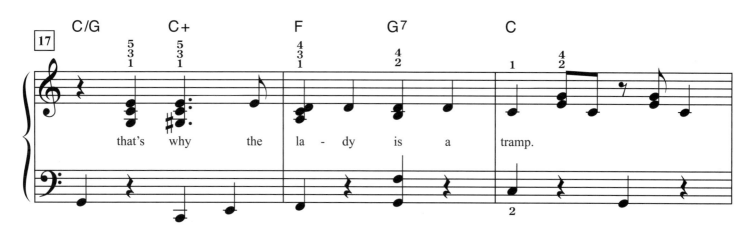

that's   why   the   la - dy   is   a   tramp.

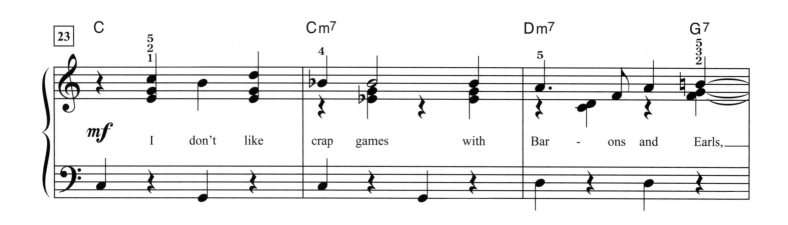

mf   I   don't   like   crap   games   with   Bar - ons   and   Earls,____

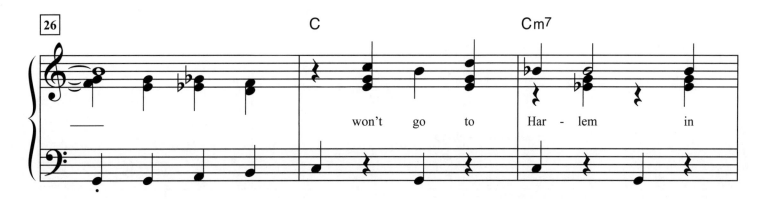

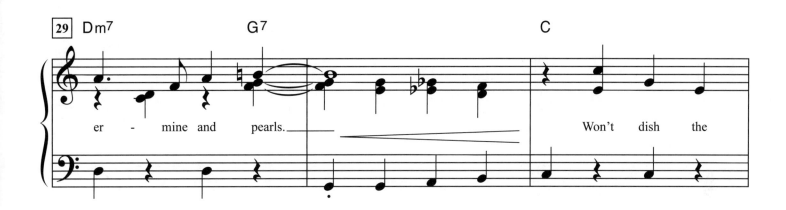

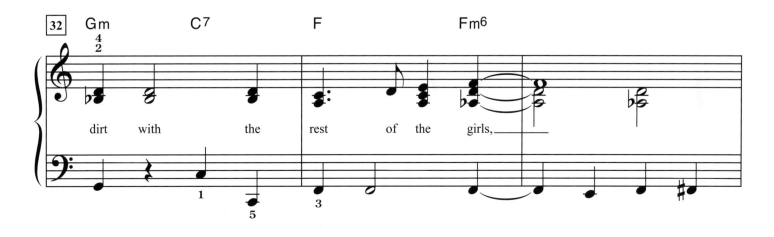

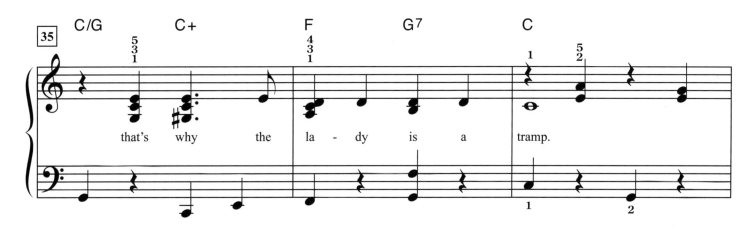

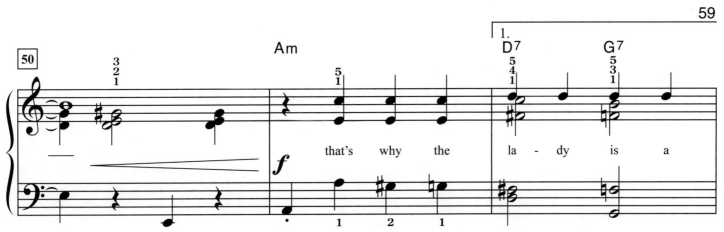

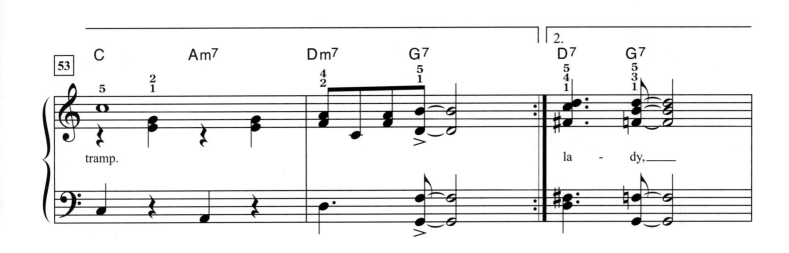

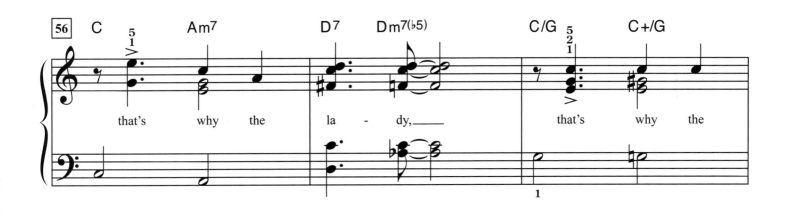

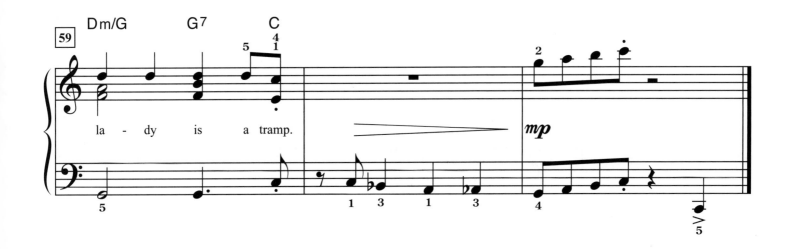

Long Ago (And Far Away)

Words by Ira Gershwin
Music by Jerome Kern
Arr. Dan Coates

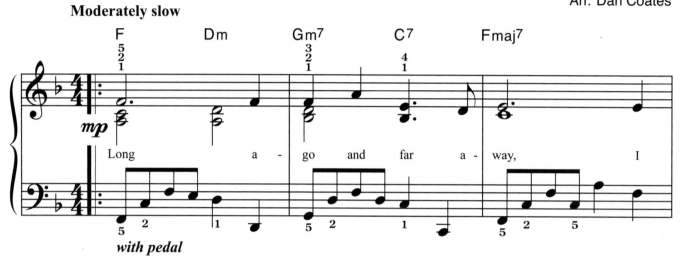

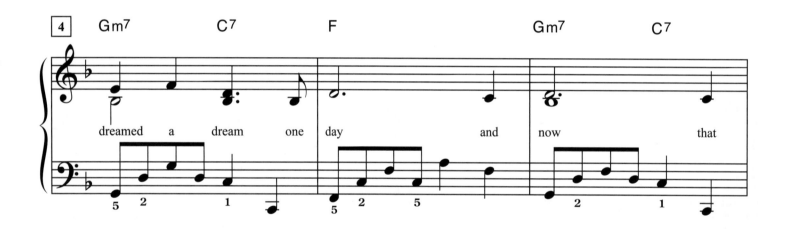

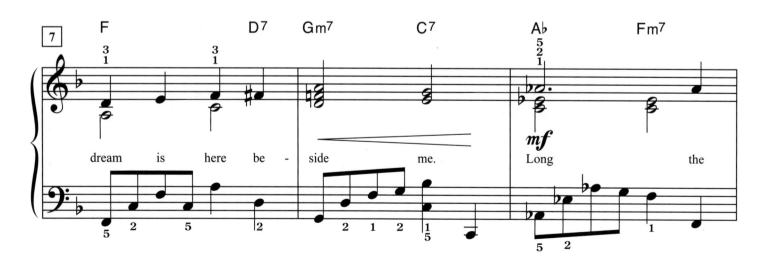

Love Is Here to Stay

Music and Lyrics by
George Gershwin and Ira Gershwin
Arr. Dan Coates

Make Someone Happy

Lyrics by Betty Comden and Adolph Green
Music by Jule Styne
Arr. Dan Coates

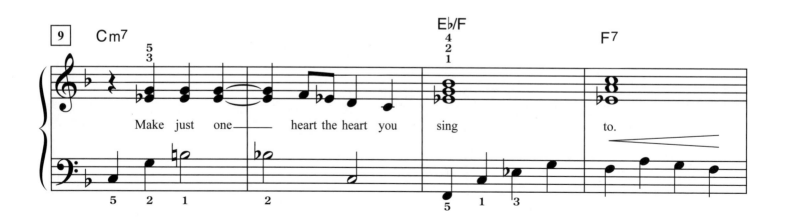

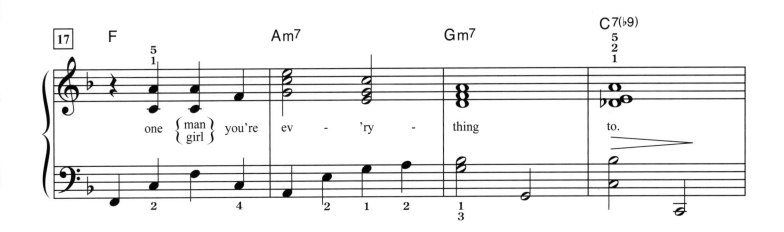

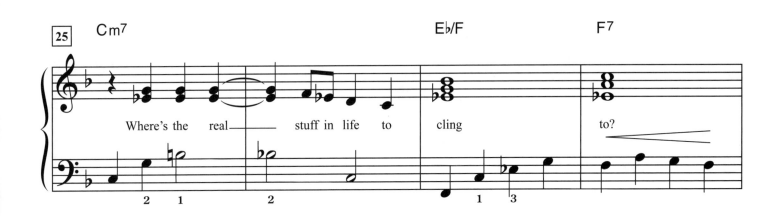

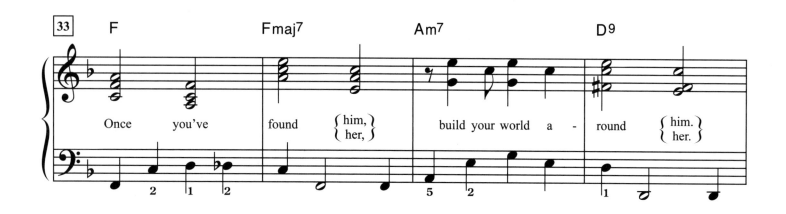

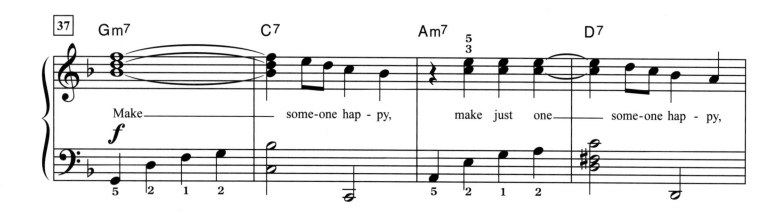

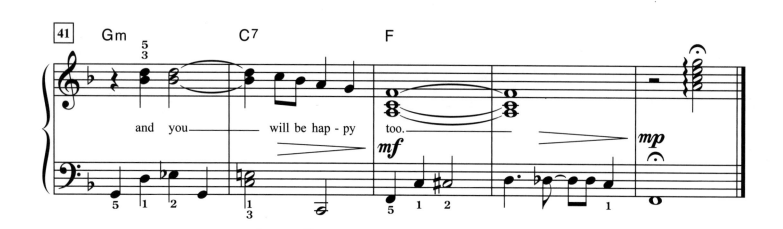

My Funny Valentine

Words by Lorenz Hart
Music by Richard Rodgers
Arr. Dan Coates

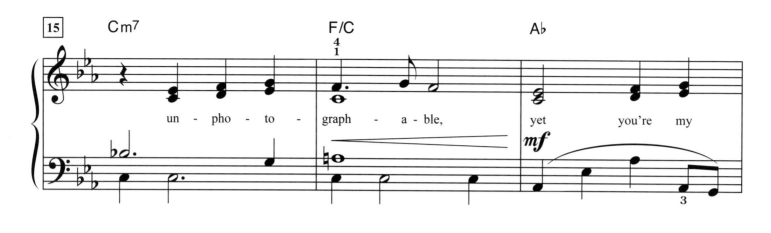

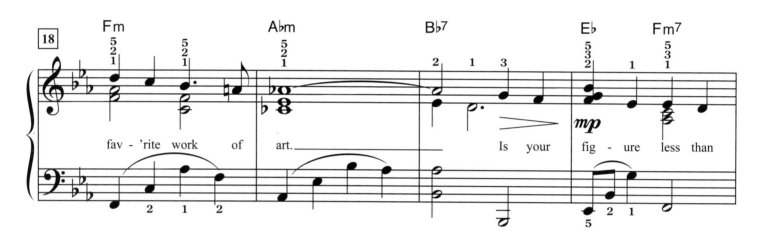

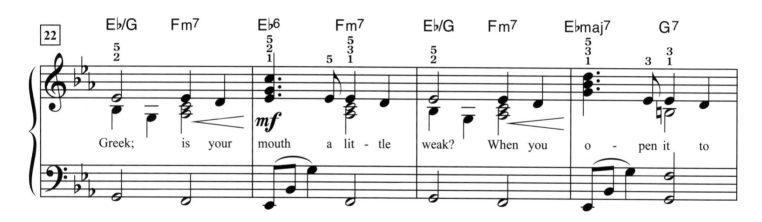

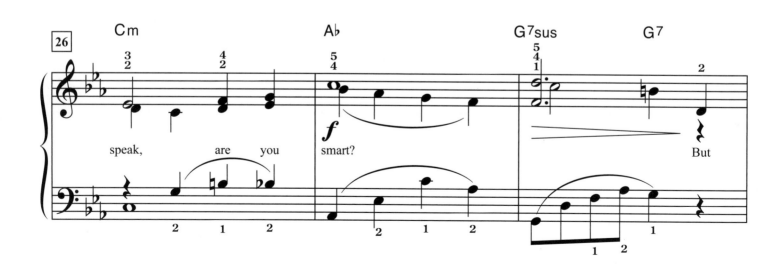

On the Street Where You Live

Words by Alan Jay Lerner
Music by Frederick Loewe
Arr. Dan Coates

The Shadow of Your Smile

Lyrics by Paul Francis Webster
Music by Johnny Mandel
Arr. Dan Coates

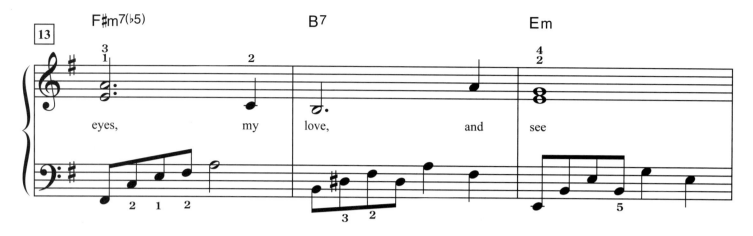

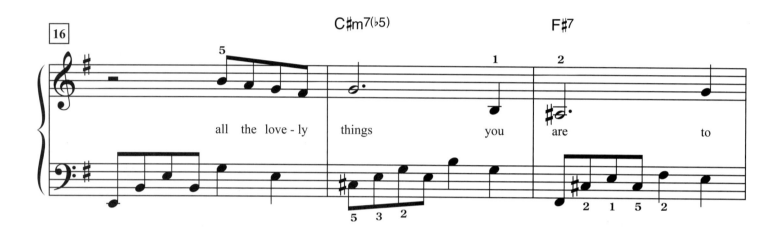

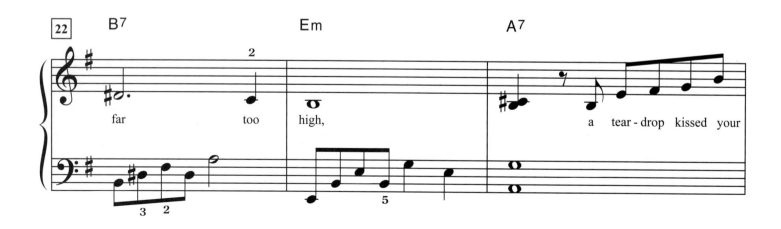

Singin' in the Rain

Music by Nacio Herb Brown
Lyric by Arthur Freed
Arr. Dan Coates

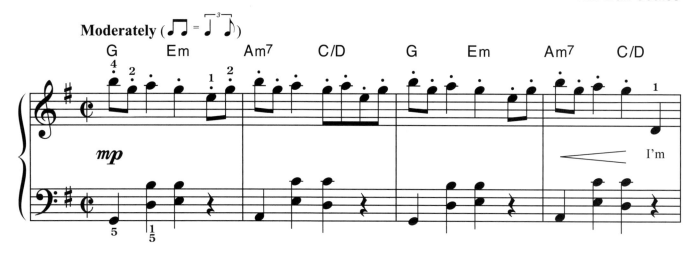

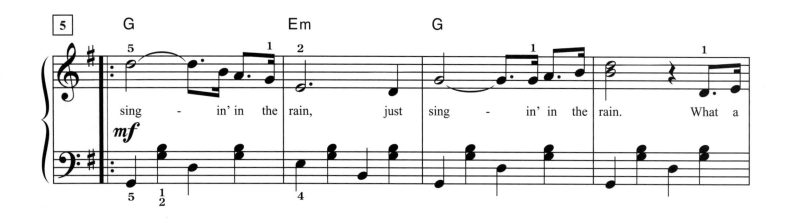

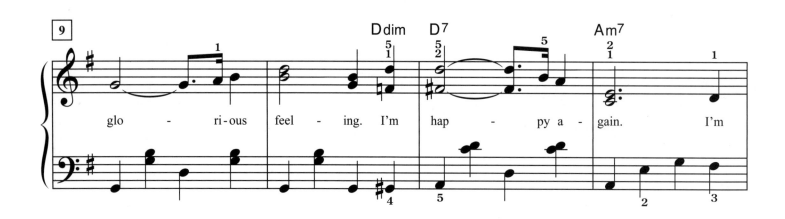

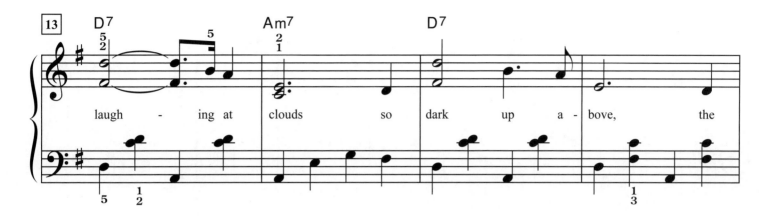

laugh - ing at clouds so dark up a - bove, the

sun's in my heart and I'm read - y for love. Let the

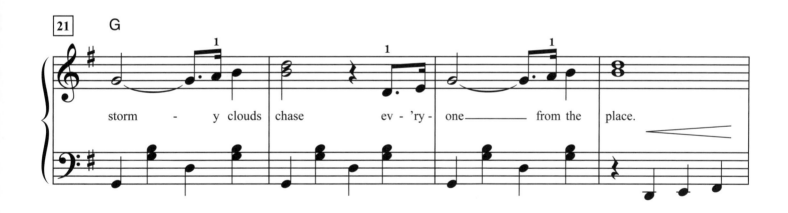

storm - y clouds chase ev - 'ry - one from the place.

Come on with the rain; I've a smile on my face. I'll

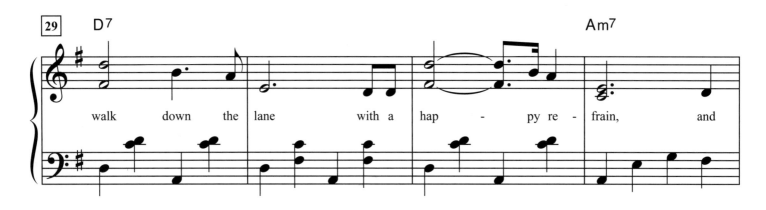

walk down the lane with a hap - py re - frain, and

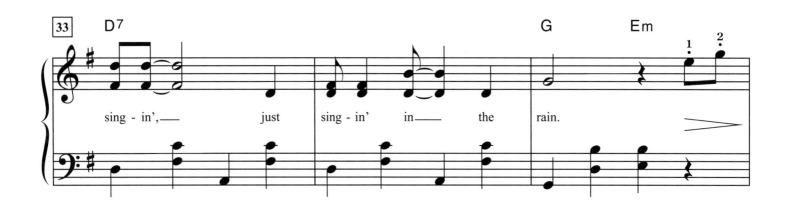

sing - in', ___ just sing - in' in ___ the rain.

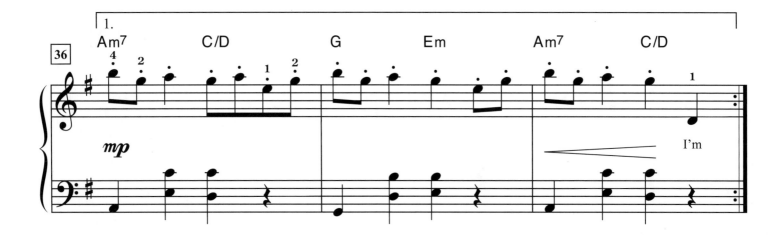

I'm

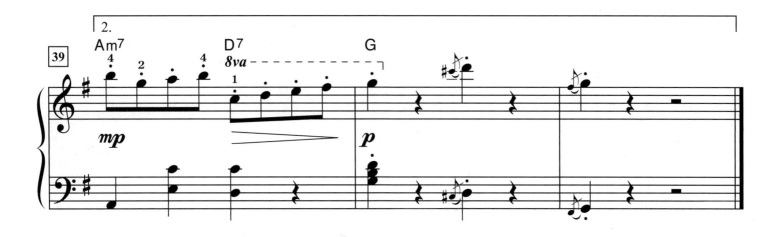

Skylark

Words by Johnny Mercer
Music by Hoagy Carmichael
Arr. Dan Coates

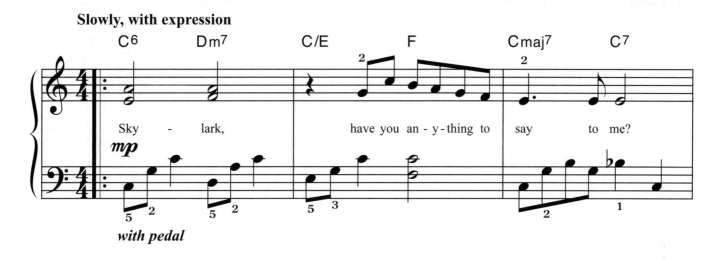

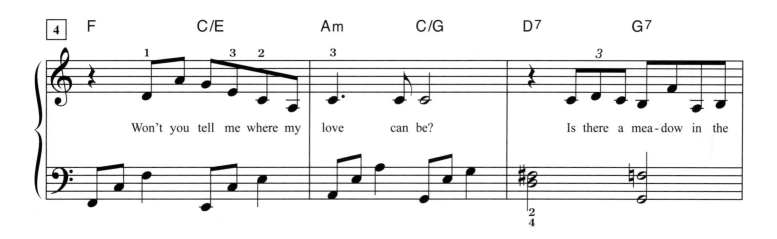

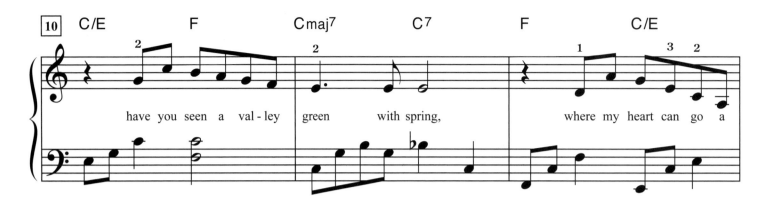

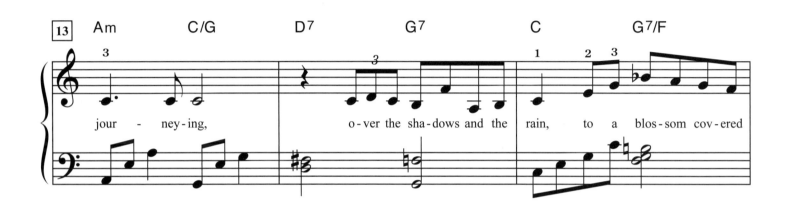

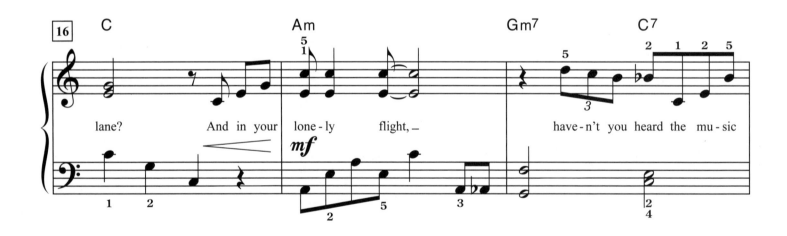

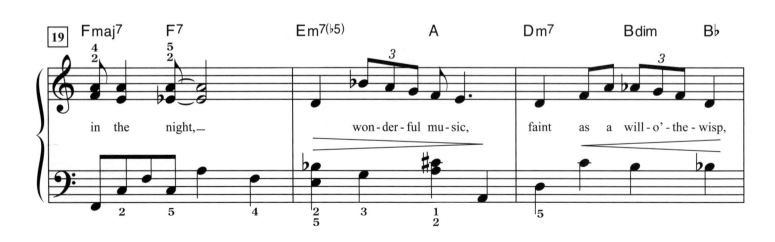

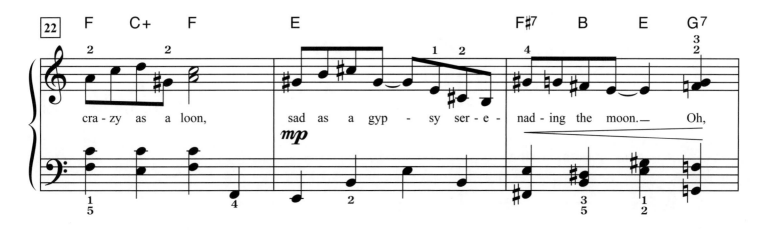

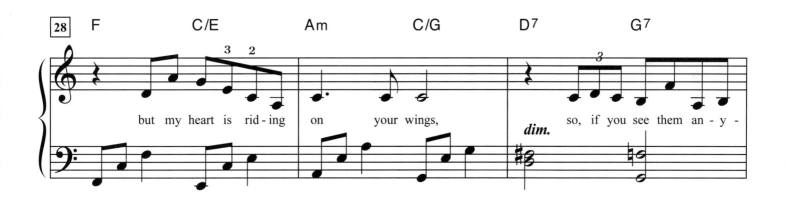

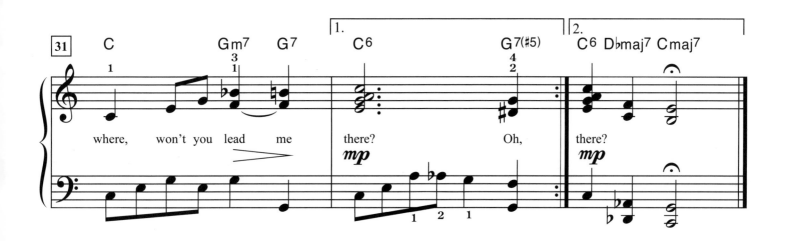

So In Love

Words and Music by Cole Porter
Arr. Dan Coates

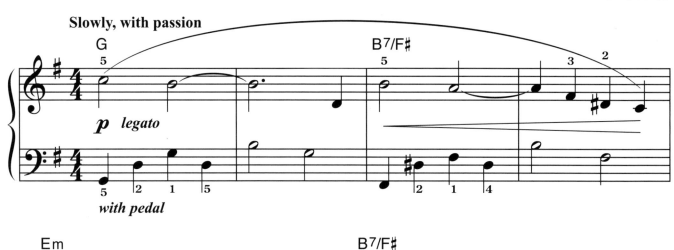

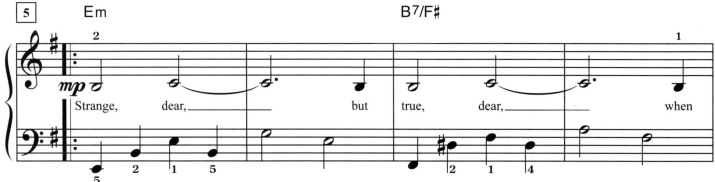

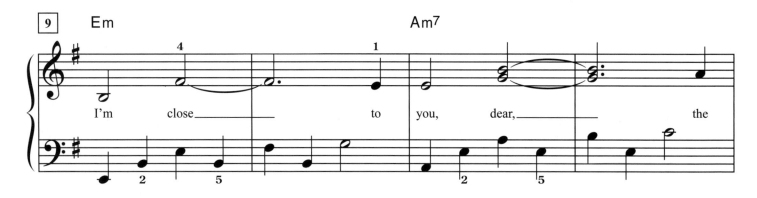

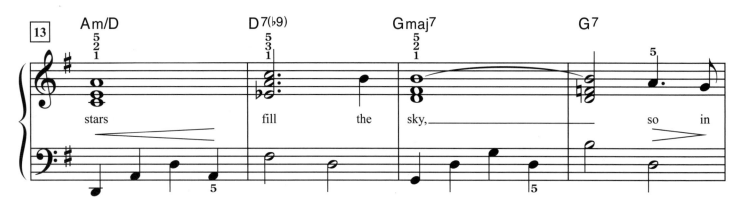

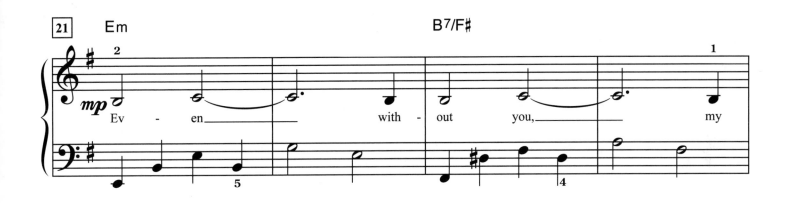

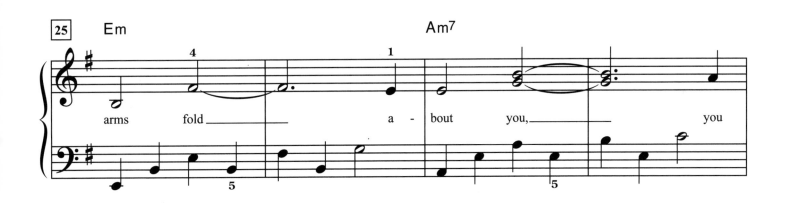

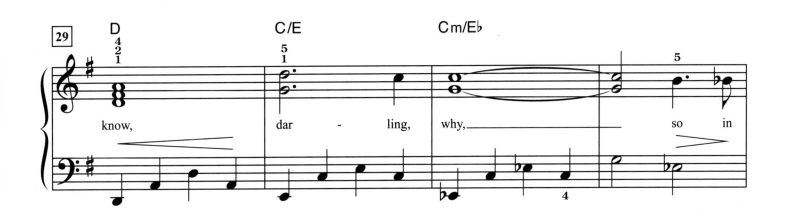

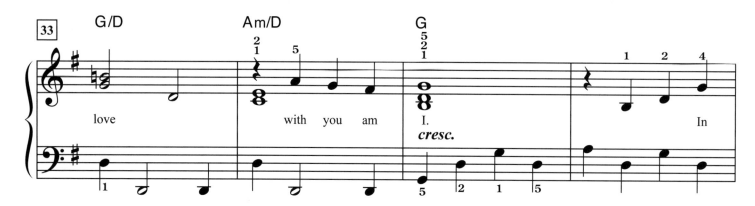

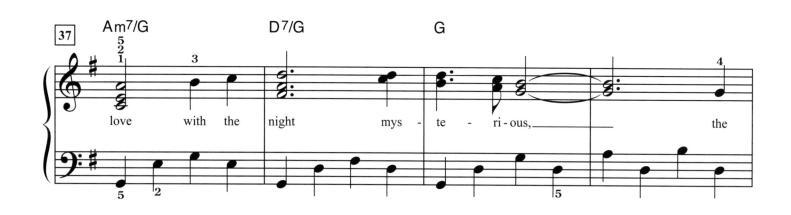

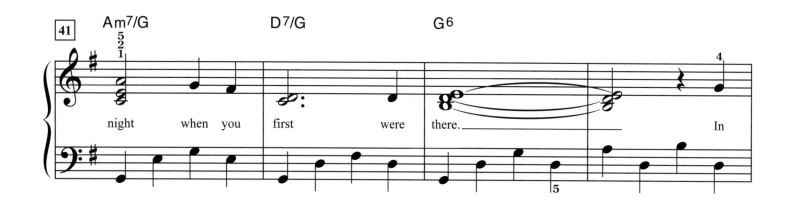

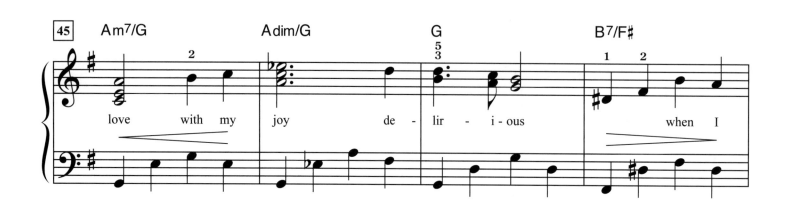

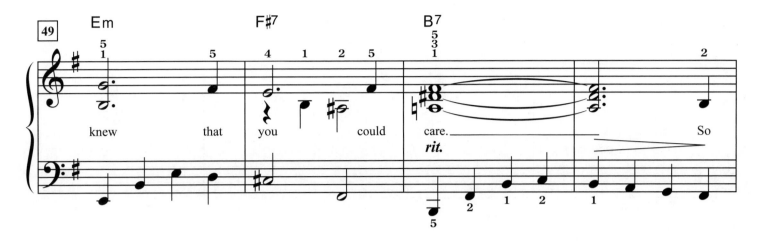

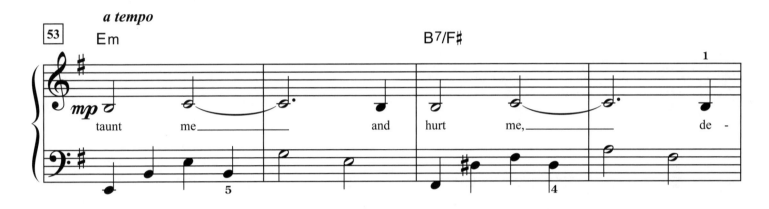

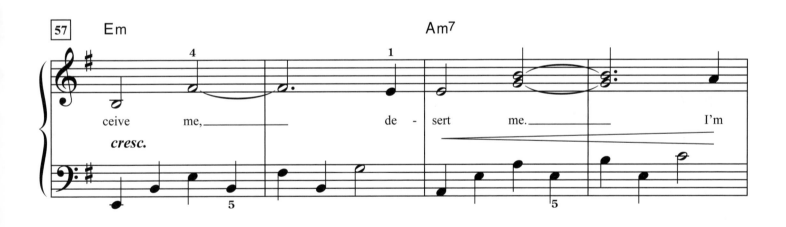

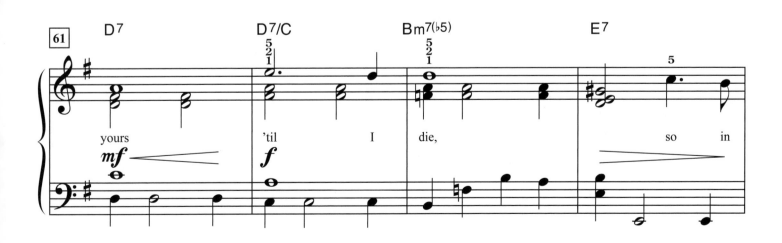

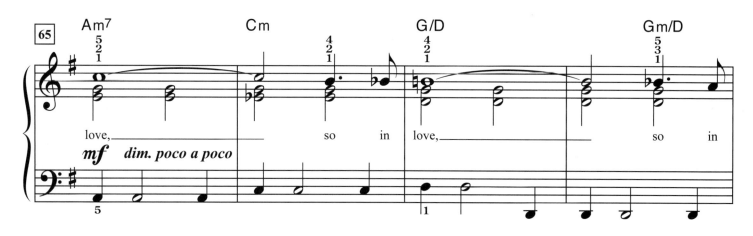

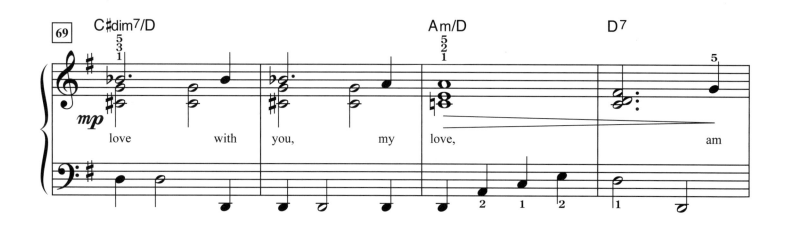

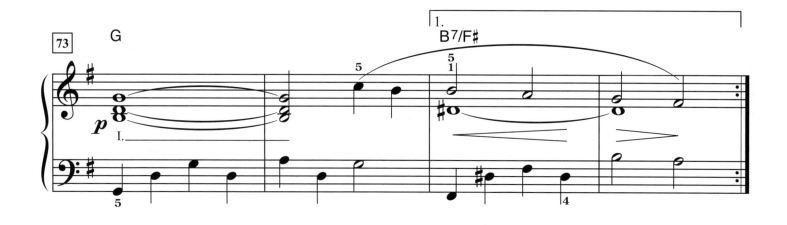

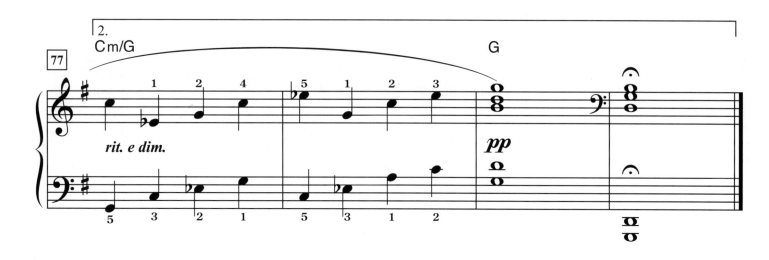

Someone to Watch Over Me

Music and Lyrics by
George Gershwin and Ira Gershwin
Arr. Dan Coates

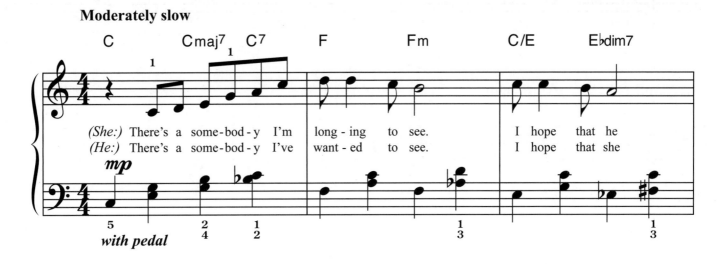

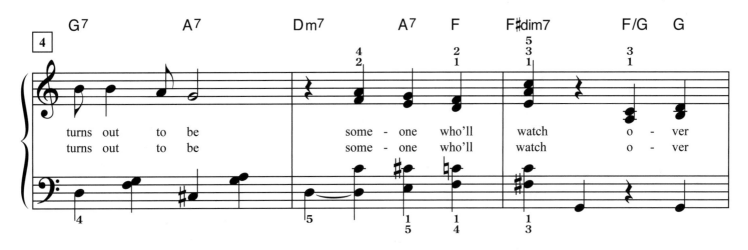

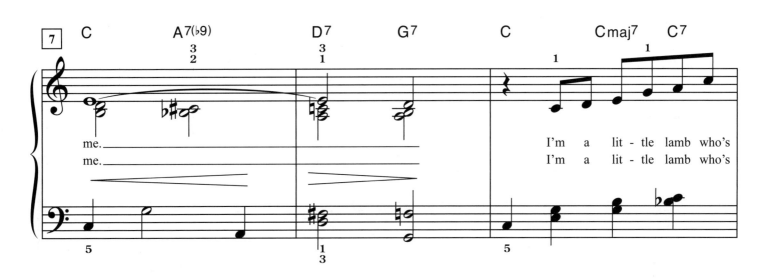

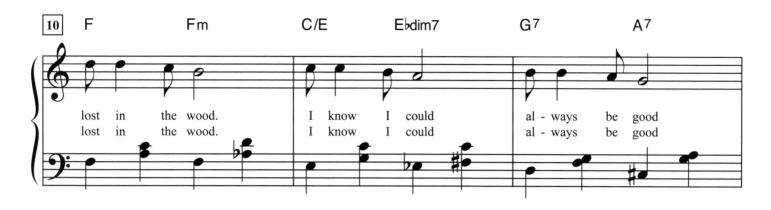

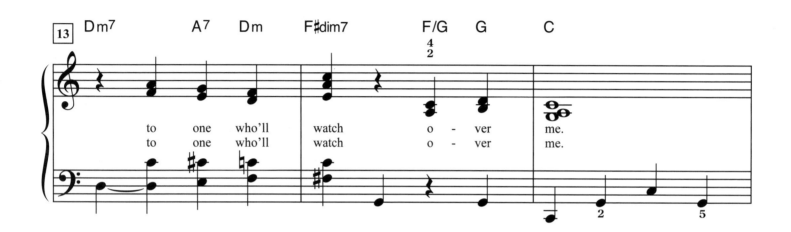

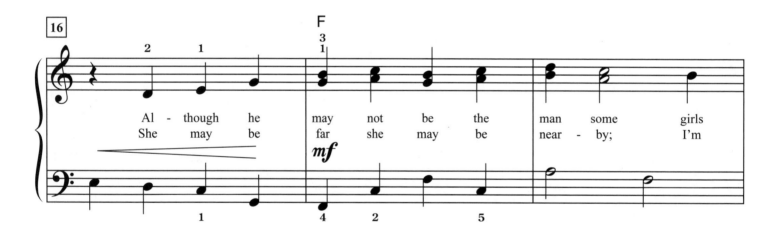

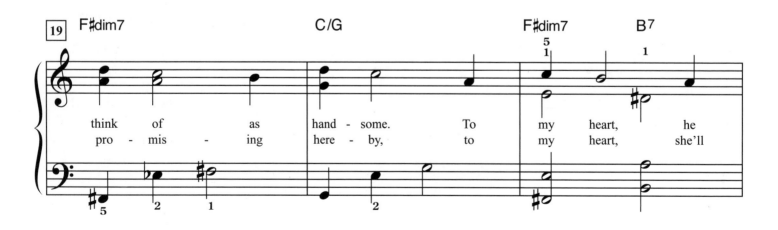

Stardust

Music by Hoagy Carmichael
Words by Mitchell Parish
Arr. Dan Coates

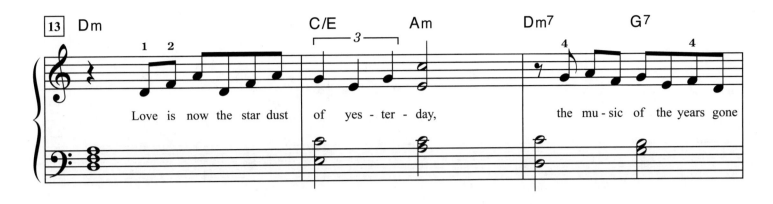

Love is now the star dust of yes - ter - day, the mu - sic of the years gone

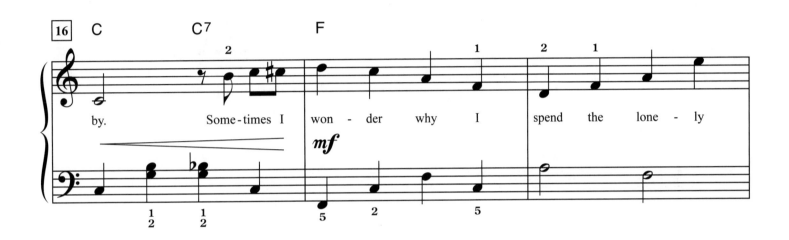

by. Some - times I won - der why I spend the lone - ly

night dream - ing of a song. The mel - o - dy

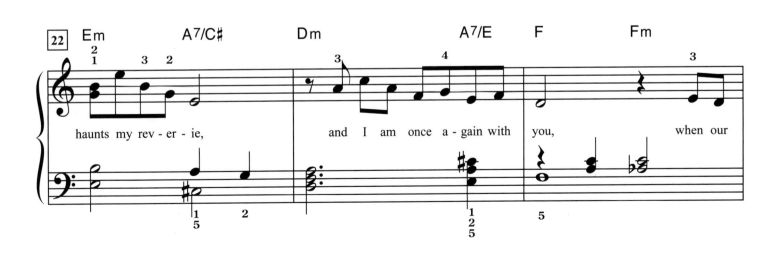

haunts my rev - er - ie, and I am once a - gain with you, when our

love was new, and each kiss an in - spir - a - tion.

But that was long a - go; now my con - so - la - tion is

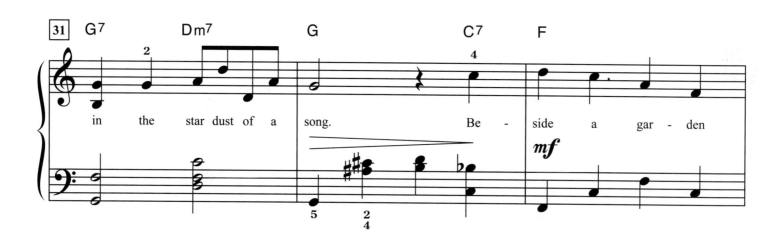

in the star dust of a song. Be - side a gar - den

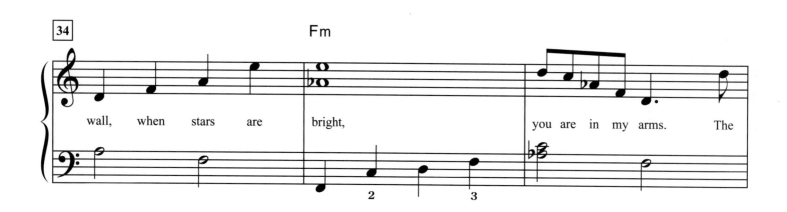

wall, when stars are bright, you are in my arms. The

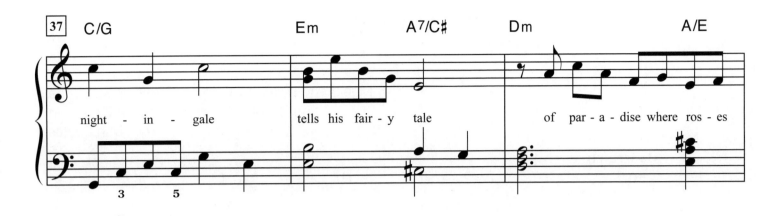

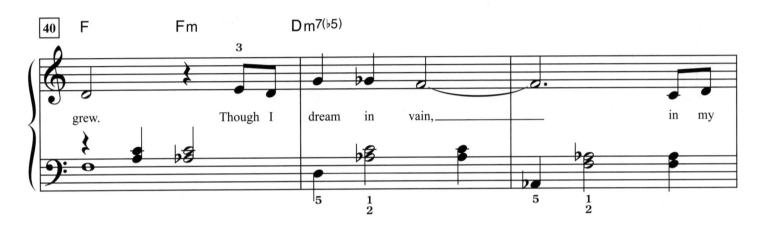

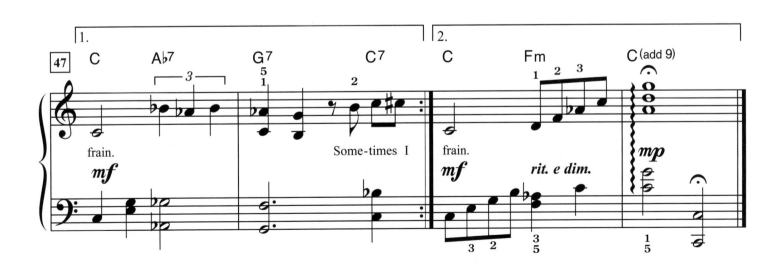

Summertime

Music and Lyrics by George Gershwin, DuBose
and Dorothy Heyward and Ira Gershwin
Arr. Dan Coates

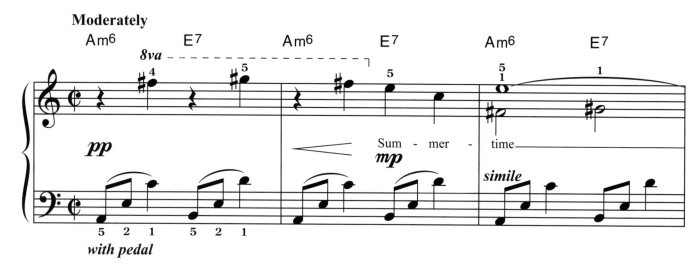

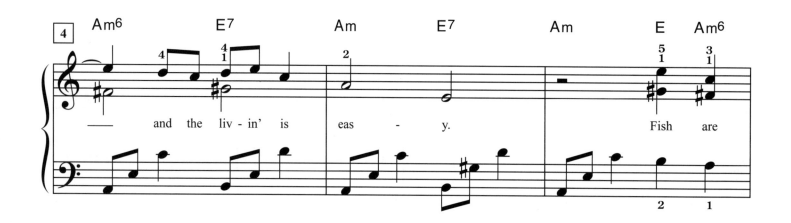

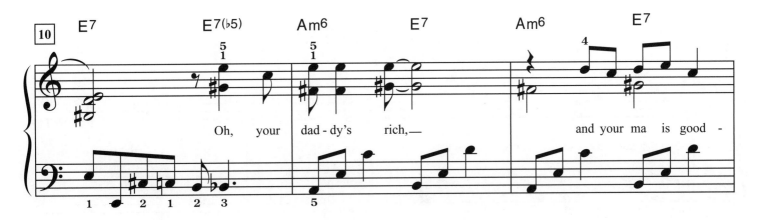

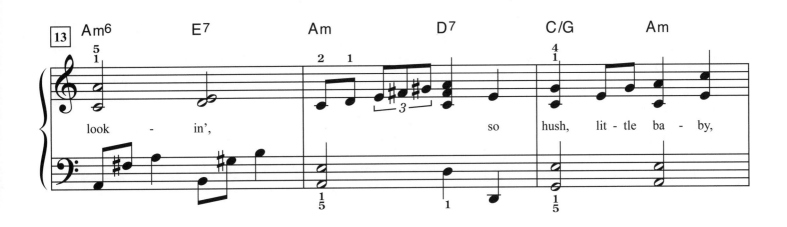

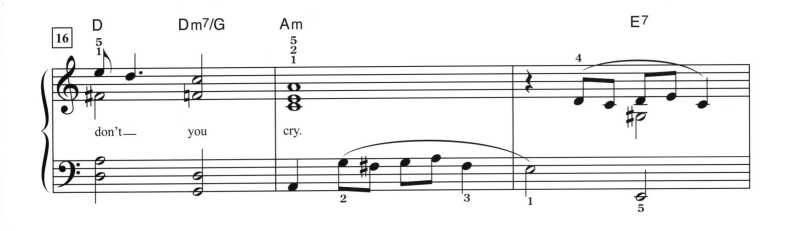

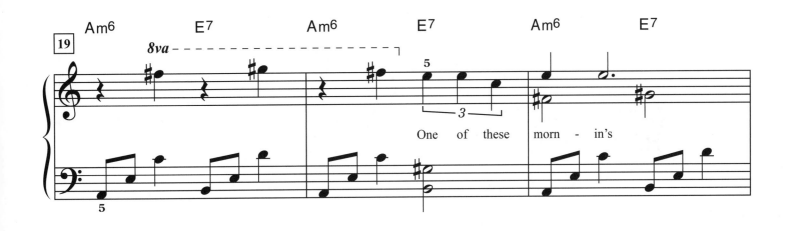

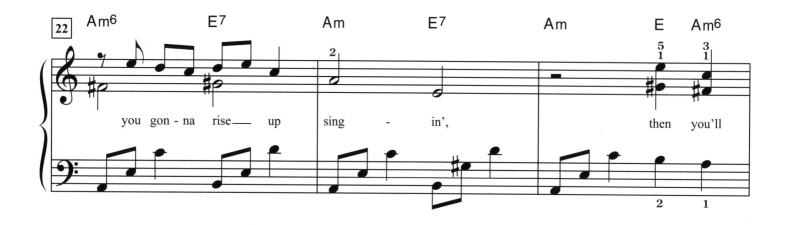

you gon - na rise—— up sing - in', then you'll

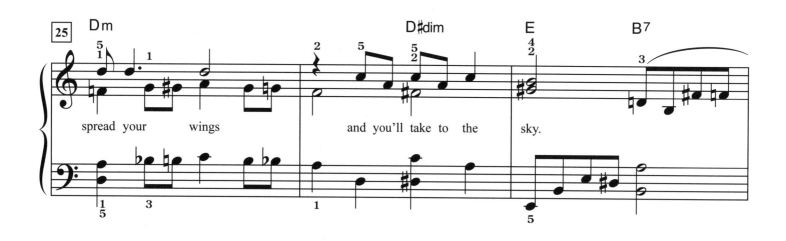

spread your wings and you'll take to the sky.

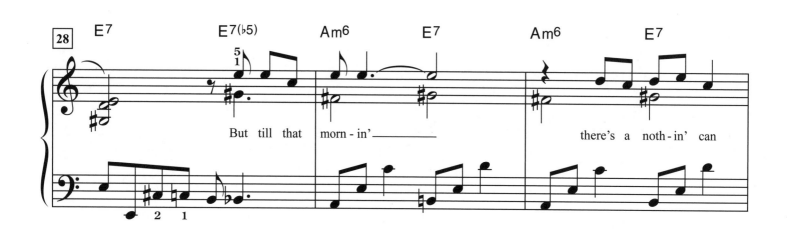

But till that morn - in'——————— there's a noth - in' can

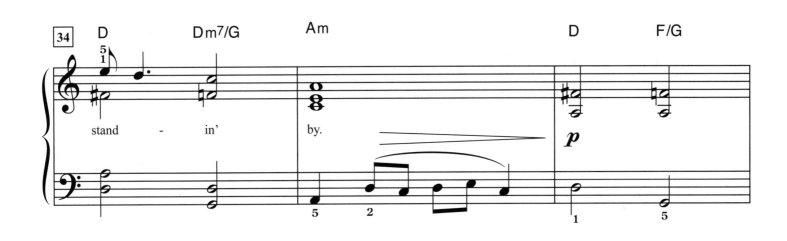

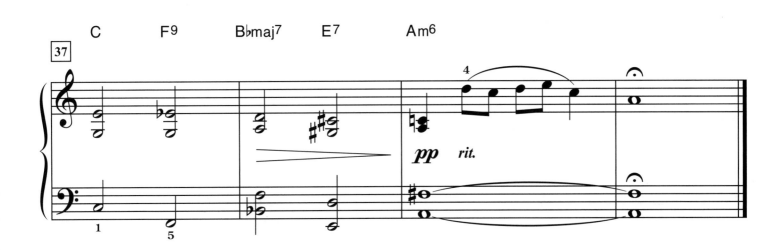

They Can't Take That Away from Me

Music and Lyrics by
George Gershwin and Ira Gershwin
Arr. Dan Coates

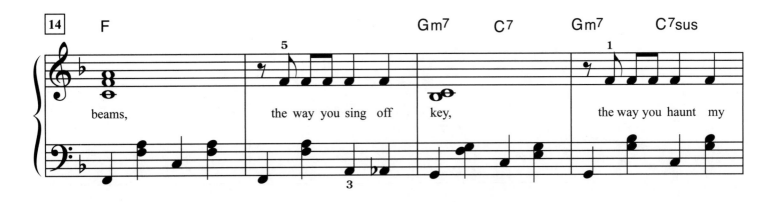

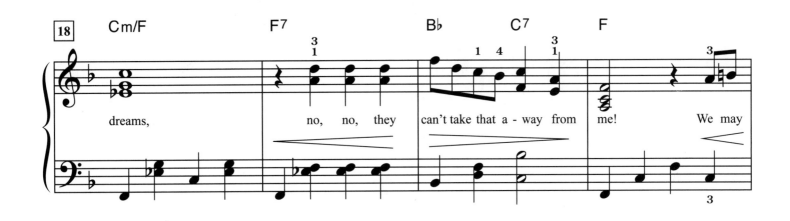

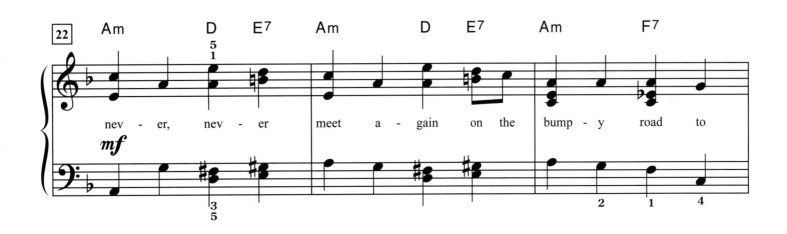

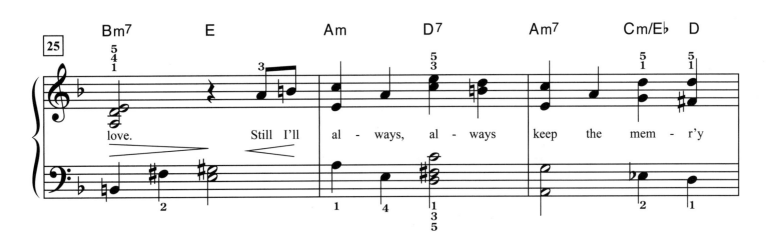

When I Fall In Love

Words by Edward Heyman
Music by Victor Young
Arr. Dan Coates

Where or When

Words by Lorenz Hart
Music by Richard Rodgers
Arr. Dan Coates

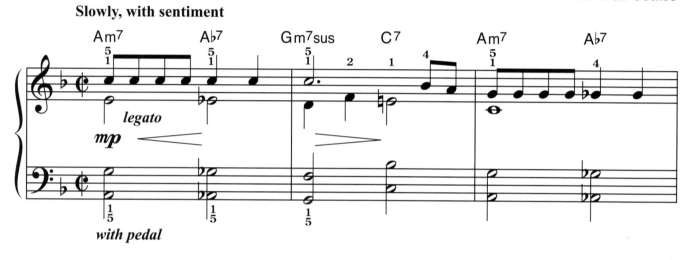

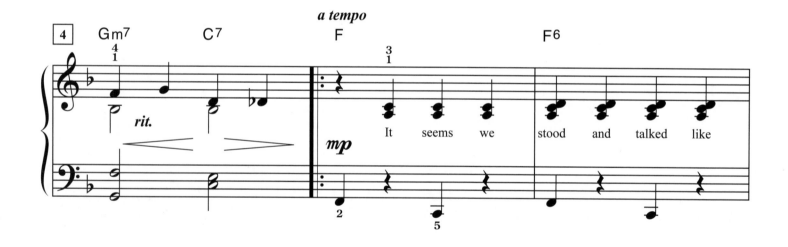

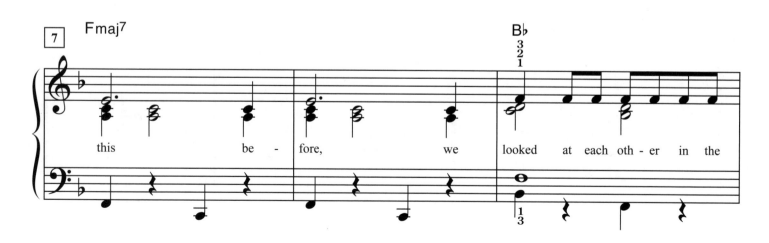

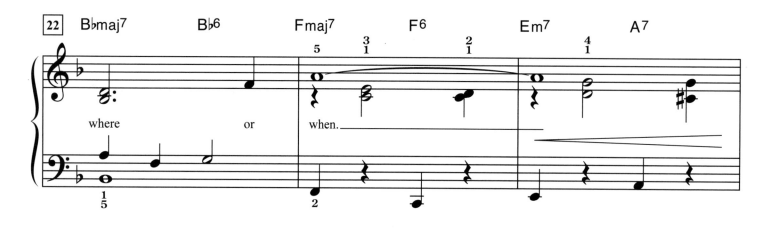

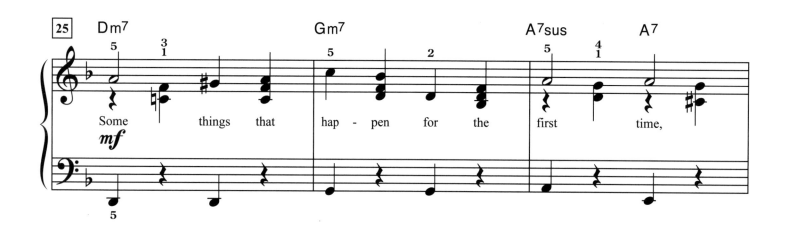

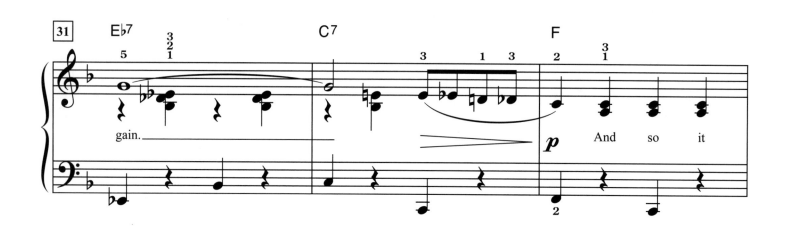

With a Song in My Heart

Words by Lorenz Hart
Music by Richard Rodgers
Arr. Dan Coates

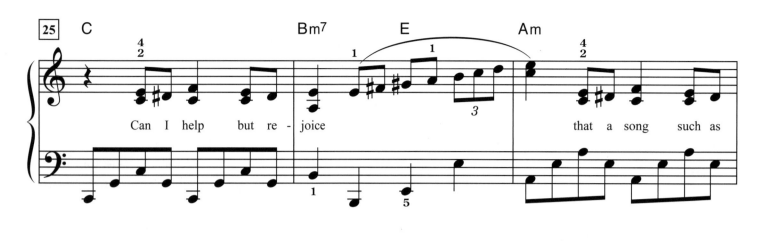

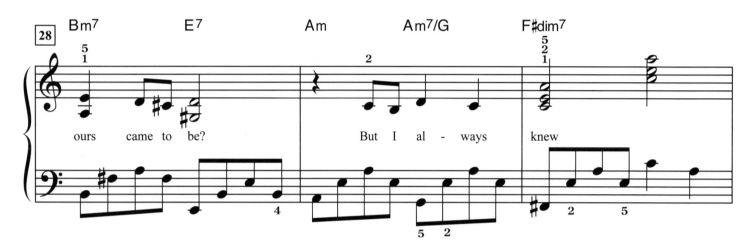

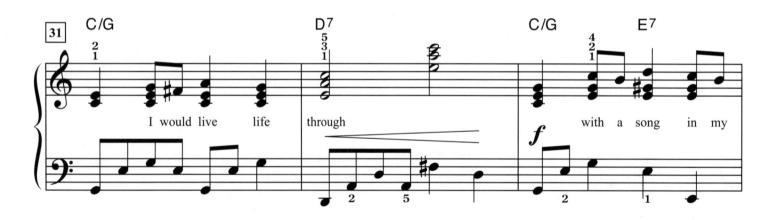

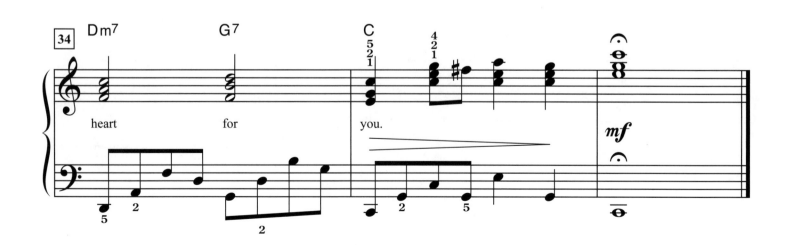

You'll Never Know

Lyrics by Mack Gordon
Music by Harry Warren
Arr. Dan Coates

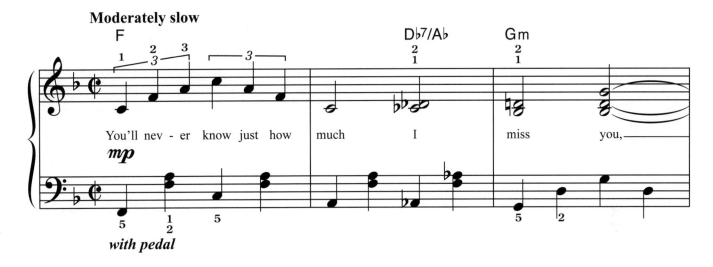

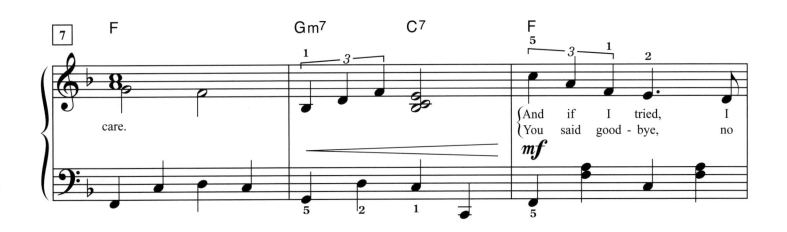

114

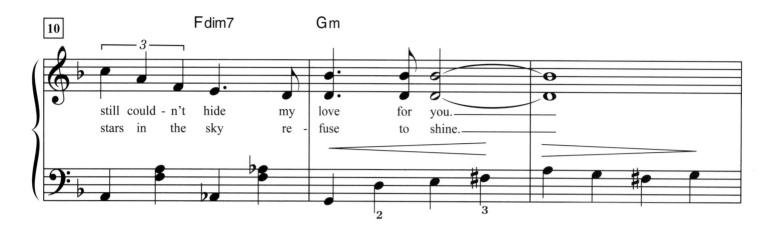

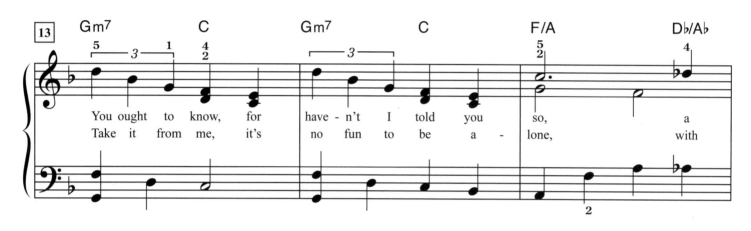

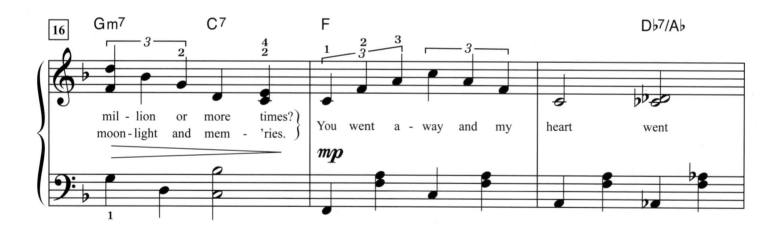

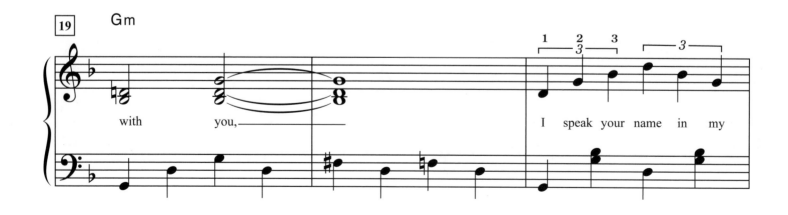

Alfred